Q: What do you call rabbits that marched in a long, sweltering Easter parade?
A: Hot, cross bunnies!

Scott was riding the subway when he noticed a man carrying a cage with a small dog in it.
"Cute pooch," Scott said.
"Got it for my wife," said the other.
"Lucky man," said Scott. "I could never find someone to make a trade like that."

"Our cat took first prize at the bird show," Mrs. Brumble boasted to her friend.
"How can that be?"
"Easy. He jumped up to the cage, reached in, and took it."

1001 GREAT PET JOKES

1,001 GREAT PET JOKES

JEFF ROVIN

A SIGNET BOOK

SIGNET
Published by the Penguin Group
Penguin Books USA Inc., 375 Hudson Street,
New York, New York 10014, U.S.A.
Penguin Books Ltd, 27 Wrights Lane,
London W8 5TZ, England
Penguin Books Australia Ltd, Ringwood,
Victoria, Australia
Penguin Books Canada Ltd, 10 Alcorn Avenue,
Toronto, Ontario, Canada M4V 3B2
Penguin Books (N.Z.) Ltd, 182–190 Wairau Road,
Auckland 10, New Zealand

Penguin Books Ltd, Registered Offices:
Harmondsworth, Middlesex, England

First published by Signet,
an imprint of New American Library,
a division of Penguin Books USA Inc.

First Printing, June, 1992
10 9 8 7 6 5 4 3 2 1

REGISTERED TRADEMARK—MARCA REGISTRADA

PRINTED IN THE UNITED STATES OF AMERICA

CONTENTS

INDIVIDUAL PETS

A MENAGERIE

INTRODUCTION

No one knows how the first pets were domesticated. Most likely they were dogs or cats
(tough to imagine anyone with a saber-
toothed tiger on a leash), though anthropolo-
gists aren't sure whether people took the animals in as hunting companions and
mousers, or whether the animals hung
around for scraps of food and eventually as-
sumed those jobs.

In any case, pets have been a part of civili-
zation since its inception—not just dogs and
cats but all *kinds* of animals, from skunks
to bees to snakes to chimpanzees to bears.
(Surely you've heard of the crooks who
stripped the house bear?)

This book contains new jokes and riddles
about *all* kinds of pets and domesticated animals, along with selected classics as well as
all-new knock-knock jokes and a menagerie
section featuring animals which aren't *exactly* pets—such as barnyard animals, lions,
and bugs—but whose jokes were too good to

pass up. (Admit it, though: Would it surprise you to learn that someone other than Michael Jackson has a giraffe or an aardvark in their backyard?)

So now, as one duck said to another: "What're you wading for?"

INDIVIDUAL PETS

CANARIES

Q: What's the difference between a miser and his pet canary?
A: One's a little cheap, the other a little cheeper.

"Hey, Timmy," Waldo cried, "didja hear about the lady who gave out canaries on Halloween?"
"No kidding!"
"Yeah! At her house, it was trick or tweet."

Q: What do you call a close race between canaries?
A: A photo finch.

Q: What do you call the canary who loses such a race?
A: A soar loser.

Gluckman screamed into the phone, "Doctor, a canary just flew down my wife's throat! What do I do?"

"I'll be right over," the doctor replied calmly. "Meanwhile, hold a slice of bread in front of her mouth, and see if you can lure it out."

Ten minutes later, the doctor arrived and found Gluckman shaking a trout over his wife's mouth.

"What on earth are you *doing*?" the doctor demanded. "I told you to use bread to get the bird out!"

"I know," said Gluckman. "But first I've got to get the cat out of there!"

"Doctor, I need help!" Wiley screamed. "I can't stop behaving like a canary!"

"I see. And how long have you had this problem?"

"Let me think. Mom laid the egg in '47. . . ."

The man walked up to the postal clerk. "Any mail for Mike Enery?"

"Nope. And none for your parakeet either."

Sitting on the perch in its cage, one canary looked down at the BMW ad in the newspaper and said to another canary, "What say we put a deposit on that car?"

Then there was the man who bought his canary for a song . . .

. . . and the bird who flew to the video store to rent *Canary Met Sally* . . .

. . . and the more literate bird who flew to the library to read *Canary Row*.

Q: What do you get if your canary flies into an electric fan?
A: Shredded tweet.

The canaries were looking out the window when a jet roared by.
"Wow," said one, "look at that sucker go!"
"Hmph," said the other. "You'd go that fast too if your tail were on fire."

Q: Why did the dummy buy birdseed?
A: He wanted to grow his own canaries.

Q: How did the canary get to the vet?
A: Flu.

Q: What did the man do when his canary was a year old?
A: He threw a birdy party.

Q: What's a canary's favorite snack?
A: Potato cheeps.

Q: How is a one-winged canary unlike a two-winged canary?
A: There's a difference of a pinion.

"There's that clod Heather," Murray said to his classmate Moe. "Y'know, she once came to my house and tripped over the canary cage. The canaries got out and were so angry they pecked at her."

"What did you do?"

"What do you think?" said Murray. "I got the birds off of Heather, flocked to get her."

Q: Where do canaries go when they have feet trouble?
A: To the chirpodist.

Q: What happened when the canary married the parrot?
A: It had offspring that knew the music *and* the words.

As they passed the pet store, the little girl looked at the parakeets in the window and said to her mother, "Look! Unripe canaries!"

Q: What was the name of the bird that played James Bond's pet?
A: Sean Canary.

Then there was the canary that was chased into the stereo system by the dog, giving new meaning to the words tweeter and woofer. . . .

"People tell me my Wilma has the most heavenly voice of any bird they've ever heard," Mrs. Finster said proudly.

Wincing from the shrill cries of the bird,

her guest said, "I believe the word they must have used is 'unearthly.' "

Q: What's small, yellow, and deadly?
A: A canary with an Uzi.

Q: What's the difference between a pet canary and one from Louisiana?
A: One's a canary encaged, the other a Cajun canary.

The boy's canary died. With his father's help, he tearfully placed it in a shoe box, dug a little grave in the backyard, and stood beside it for a moment in silence.

"Don't you think you should say something?" the father said.

The boy nodded, and said, "I do this in the name of the Father, the Son—and in the hole he goes."

After a spirited auction, Marvin went up to the auctioneer.

"I just paid a fortune for this parrot. Do you guarantee he'll talk?"

"Absolutely. Who do you think was bidding against you?"

CATS

What do you call a cat that . . .
   . . . is always mad? *Angory*.
   . . . is always in a hurry? *Rushin' blue*.
   . . . has its own talk show? *Abyssinian Hall*.
   . . . has a communicable disease? *Sia-measles*.
   . . . likes Buddy Holly songs? *Calico Boy*.
   . . . lives in the desert? *Sandy Claws*.
   . . . has a wicked uppercut? *Muhammad Alleycat*.
   . . . sucks on lemons? *A sourpuss*.

Q: When is it time for a cat to move out of the house?
A: When the place goes to the dogs.

Q: What does the Flash put in his cat's litter box?
A: Quicksand.

Q: What's the difference between expensive floor coverings and a contented cat?

A: The first are Persian rugs, the other purrs on rugs.

Q: What's the difference between a cat and a comma?
A: A cat has claws at the end of its paws, and a comma's a pause at the end of a clause.

THE MORAL OF THE TAIL IS . . .

After listening to the cats crying in his backyard for two nights in a row, Melvin decided to buy a dog.

At last he had a restful night. As he said to his wife when he awoke the following morning, "No mews is good news."

Pokey the farm cat was as slow as could be, especially compared to his littermates, who did everything quickly. The cats drank their milk particularly fast, and always ended up with a bellyache. While they'd roll around in pain, Pokey would come over and drink slowly, getting far more than his kitty siblings. As he said to the other kittens each and every time, "He who laps last, laps best."

Pokey's slowness was an advantage in another way too. One day he and his fleet sister Sassy were out playing in the barn. A mare got out of her stall, and while Pokey walked a safe distance behind the escaped horse, Sassy got in front of its drumming hooves. The mare trampled her, and as Pokey said after pulling his dazed sister to safety, "Don't you know you should *never* put the cat before the horse?"

Q: What do you call newborn kittens which keep getting passed from owner to owner?
A: A chain litter.

Marvin was sick of the neighbor's cat roaming through his yard and getting into the garbage. Since he didn't want to get a dog, he went to the local pet obedience trainer, a Chinese gentleman named Mr. Tung, and asked for help.

Mr. Tung came over and placed a piece of fish in a cage. When the cat walked in, he slammed the door behind it. Mr. Tung told Marvin he'd train the cat to stay out of his yard, then return it to the neighbor.

The next day, Marvin's neighbor went looking for his pet. When he noticed Marvin whistling with uncharacteristic glee, he knew *something* bad had to have happened.

"All right, Marvin," the neighbor said. "What's the matter?"

Grinning broadly, Marvin said, "What's the matter? Tung's got your cat."

Q: What did the owner say after her cat got its tail caught in the garbage disposal?
A: "It won't be long now!"

Mrs. Fiftal said to her husband, "My mother said she's going to leave at once unless we do something about the mice in her room."

Mr. Fiftal got up.

"Where are you going?" his wife asked.

"To shoot the cat," he answered.

Then there was the NFL scout who came looking for the tomcat that had covered twenty yards in half a minute . . .

. . . and the cat who ate worms and then waited by the pond with baited breath.

The baggage handlers at Intercontinental Airlines were horrified when they unloaded a cage and found that the cat inside was dead. The cat was a rare English breed and, fearful of a lawsuit, the airline president notified the owner that the cat had been sent to France by accident, but would be back within hours. Then he had a plane fly to Europe, locate another cat with the same markings, pay a tidy fortune for it, and return to the United States.

After slipping the dead cat's jewel-encrusted collar on the new animal, the president himself brought it to the owner's door.

The woman's eyes went wide. "Why, that's not my Fluffy!" she cried.

The president's knees shook. "W-what makes you say that?"

"Because Fluffy died while we were on vacation. I was having her flown home for burial."

Mrs. Pepperwinkle was devastated when her cat Mary expired. She wanted to give it a proper funeral, but both the Catholic and Protestant churches in her neighborhood refused to bury a cat.

In desperation, the woman turned to the synagogue and asked the rabbi if he would say a few words at the cat's funeral.

"Mrs. Pepperwinkle," the rabbi said, "for one thing, we do not believe in burying animals. For another, you're not even Jewish—"

"I intend to donate a half million dollars in Mary's name to any house of worship which will accept her," the woman interrupted.

"—on the other hand, I do believe the cat *is* Jewish. . . ."

Mr. Franklin was unable to keep from running over the cat as it bolted through a bush and darted in front of his car. Picking up the poor limp animal, he carried it to the house and rang the bell. A white-haired old woman answered the door.

"I'm sorry," said Mr. Franklin, "but I'm afraid I've run over your cat. I'd like to replace it."

"Certainly," the woman replied. "How are you at catching mice?"

The football stadium was infested with cats, but no one minded: They kept the mice away. One day, a cat chased a mouse up the scoreboard and over the side. The mouse was able to hold on, but the cat was not.

As it happened, Abramowicz was going out for a pass at just that moment. Noticing the cat plummeting toward the field, he poured on the speed, extended his arms, and caught it on the tips of his fingers. When he hauled it to his chest, the crowd, watching the incredible display, jumped to their feet and cheered.

And as he entered the end zone, the ecstatic if not too bright Abramowicz enthusiastically spiked the cat.

Mr. Jenkins's tomcat Buster had a nasty habit of howling each time he wooed a lady cat. After several nights, his owner had him neutered.

A few days later, one of the neighbors stopped by to see Jenkins.

"It's been a lot quieter since you had the cat fixed," said the neighbor. "I'll bet he's just loafing around now, getting fat."

"Oh, no," Mr. Jenkins replied. "He still goes out each night."

"Really? What for."

Mr. Jenkins replied, "These days, he's a consultant."

Mr. Saffi asked a friend, "Did you ever see the Catskill Mountains?"
"No," said the neighbor. "Just mice."

The randy tomcat saw a lovely miss on the other side of a picket fence. He simply had to meet her and, after a mighty leap in which he barely cleared the stakes, he waited while the lady cat sashayed over.
"That was an impressive jump," she said. "Want to go somewhere and smooch?"
"No point in that now," the tomcat replied wincing. "The fence was a wee bit higher than I thought."

Then there was the cat who won a milk-drinking contest by three laps . . .

. . . and the old woman who kept taking in stray cats due to her add-a-puss complex . . .

. . . and poor little Caryn, who got a kitten and let it nap with her beside the fireplace. After a few minutes, the cat began to purr and Caryn leapt up screaming, "Mama, come quickly! Kitty's beginning to boil!"

Three salesmen—an Englishman, a German, and a Pole—stopped at an inn. Also lodging there was a mean, brutish-looking man whose wife was charming and beautiful . . . so much so that the salesmen resolved to try to woo her as soon as her husband went to bed.

The men listened from their room down the hall. They heard the couple enter their bedroom, and when the husband began to snore the Englishman set out toward the room.

As he neared, the floorboards creaked and the husband awoke, startled.

"Who's out there?" he yelled.

"Meooooowww!" said the Englishman, and beat a hasty retreat.

Next, the German tried to reach the room. Once again the floorboards creaked and the husband woke.

"Who's *there*?" he screamed.

"Meooooow!" the German answered, and hurried away.

Then it was the Pole's turn. Creeping over, he too caused the floorboards to creak.

"Who's there?" shouted the husband.

"It's just me, the cat," said the Pole.

The man took his poor sick Siamese into the vet. "Doctor, will you treat my cat?"

"Certainly not. You'll have to pay like everyone else."

Q: What's the difference between people and cats?

A: To a person, Saudi Arabia's Nefud desert is 400,000 square miles of oil. To a cat, it's 400,000 square miles of kitty litter.

Mrs. Finch said to Mr. Finch, "Did you put the cat out?"

"Hell," said Mr. Finch, "I didn't even know it was on fire."

A woman phoned the vet, frantic. "Doctor, my cat just swallowed a roll of film! What should I do?"

"Stay calm," the doctor replied, "and we'll see what develops."

Q: What rock and roll group does every cat hope to avoid?
A: Three Dog Night.

Freddie told a pal, "My cat lived for two weeks on a single can of cat food."

"Amazing," said the friend. "How'd you keep him from getting off?"

Then there was the feline who robbed Burger Kings across the state and earned quite a reputation as a cat burgerlar . . .

. . . and the cat who got to play professional tennis after someone helped him get into the racket . . .

. . . and the cat who wanted to play poker because he heard he'd get to put a little something into the kitty.

Q: What do you call a paramedic cat?
A: A first aid kit.

Q: What do you call a German cat who's had a run-in with a lawn mower?
A: A cat o' *nein* tails.

Then there was the dummy who waited all night for the cat to come in so he could put him out . . .

. . . and the ASPCA report which declared that there are ten million overweight cats—and those are only round figures . . .

. . . and the foreigner who was learning English and teaching it to the rest of his family. Unfortunately, he didn't quite get the hang of it. After learning that a *narrative* was a "tale," and *douse* meant to "put out," he went home and told his daughter to catch the cat by the narrative and douse it.

Diana brought the kitten home for her five-year-old daughter Vanessa. No sooner had she left the two alone than she heard the girl crying.

"What's wrong?" Diana said as she rushed into the playroom.

"Kitty bit me!" said the girl.

"Poor girl," said the woman. "But Kitty's just a baby—she doesn't *know* that that hurts."

A few minutes later, Diana heard the cat shriek and ran back to the playroom. "What happened this time?" she asked.

Vanessa replied, "Now she knows."

Stella visited her sister Myrtle in the country. "My, but you have an awful lot of cats around here," Stella said. "Why don't you shoo them?"

Myrtle said, "Because, dearie, cats are *meant* to go barefoot."

The woman named her cat Love because it was so affectionate. One night, Love failed to come home and the woman went looking for her. Because she was running around frantically, dressed only in a bathrobe, a police officer pulled up next to her.

"What are you doing?" the policeman asked.

"I'm out here looking for Love," the woman replied.

The officer arrested her on the spot.

Q: What do you call a cat you get at the animal shelter?
A: A freeline.

The mother cat yelled through the window, "Son, what are you doing out there?"

"Chasing a mouse, Mom!"

"How many times have I told you not to play with your food?"

Q: What's the difference between a silvery gray cat and an ice pack?
A: One's a chinchilla, while the other cools the top of the head.

Marcy was surprised to find her cat sleeping in the refrigerator.

"What are you doing in there?" she asked.

"Isn't this a Westinghouse?" the cat replied.

"Yes—"

"Well," said the smart aleck cat, "I'm westing."

Kathy and her mother were glancing down at the old cat.

"Do you think kitty was on Noah's Ark?" Kathy asked.

"I don't think so," her mother said with a smile.

"Then how come she didn't drown?"

Then there was the motel proprietor who needed a mouser and advertised for a cat that was inn-experienced.

Mark was playing at Ryan's house.

"How old's your little sister?" Mark asked as the girl stumbled by.

"She's a little over a year old."

"Hah!" said Mark. "I've got a cat who's just a *month* old, and he can walk better'n her!"

Ryan said, "That's 'cause he's got twice as many legs!"

"I haven't got no pets," the teacher said to the class. "What should I do to correct that?"

Barbara raised her hand. "Buy a kitty?"

Then there was the pet shop owner who gave kittens to needy children while letting the rest of the world go buy . . .

. . . and the puss who went to work for Xerox and became a copycat.

Eloise said to May, "What makes you think your cat is a carpenter?"

May said, "When I went to give her a bath, she made a bolt for the door."

The vet stroked the cat's back. "No need to worry about this fella," he told the owner. "He'll live to be fifteen."

"But doctor—he *is* fifteen."

"See?" said the vet. "What did I tell you?"

Q: What would you call a baby cat born in Yugoslavia with one ear, no tail, and tawny fur?

A: A kitten.

Q: What's the difference between a fly and a cat?

A: You can't zip a cat.

Q: What do cats and dogs have in common?

A: s.

Then there was the tailor who killed his cat by letting it out . . .

. . . and the wimpy cat who couldn't even lick a bowl of milk.

The agitated woman called the police. "My kitty just fell down the well! What should I do?"

The desk sergeant replied, "Try a book."

"A book?"

"Yeah . . . on how to raise cats."

Later, another agitated woman phoned the police. "You've got to help me! I've lost a black cat with one ear, named Xavier."

"And what's the other ear called?" the desk sergeant asked.

Meredith said to her friend, "I just read that somewhere there's a cat giving birth every *second*."

"Goodness," said the friend. "Someone should find her and stop her!"

"That cat is pretty dirty," Mrs. Mulvey said to the little girl.

"Yes," the girl said, "and she's even prettier clean."

Horace knocked on the door.

"Hello, madam. I'm collecting for homeless cats—"

"Sorry," the woman replied, "but the dog chases them away."

"My mom says we're getting a cat for Christmas," Tanya told her friend.
"No kidding? We're having a turkey like we do every year."

"That cat's howling is driving me mad!" screamed Mr. Ogan.
"You don't need driving," said his wife.

Q: What did they call Wyatt Earp's kitten?
A: A posse cat.

"I've got to write a composition on my cat," said Rue.
"Great," said her brother. "I'll hold it still while you get the pen."

"My cat had a fight with a porcupine," Evelyn told a friend.
"Who won?"
Evelyn said, "The porcupine did, on points."

Q: What kind of a tree will a cat never climb?
A: A dogwood.

Q: What opera did the cat sing after snaring a bird?
A: *Aida.*

Q: What do cats enjoy eating as a side dish?
A: Mice-a-Roni.

And what about the rich cats that made a Persian-to-Persian call . . .

. . . or the ones that kept the neighborhood safe through claw enforcement . . .

. . . or the cat who collected string to play with and, over the years, had a ball . . .

. . . or the cat who got into a *phssssst* fight?

Michael said to his friend, "Can you believe it? I didn't have an umbrella, but I followed my cat down the streets and through backyards and didn't get a drop of water on me!"
"How can that be?"
"It wasn't raining," Michael replied.

Ilsa told her brother, "The cat got caught in the lawn mower and its left side got chopped off!"
"Is it dead?" the boy asked.
"No," Ilsa said with a shrug. "It's all right."

Two hillbillies, Ernie and Bert, were walking through the woods, looking for squirrels. Suddenly Bert saw foliage rustle, cried "I seed something move!" raised his squirrel gun, and fired.

Turns out it wasn't a squirrel but their pet puss, which had just eaten a squirrel. Not wanting to waste the meat, the hillbillies had feline pie that night. As Ernie told their mom, "That's what happens when a squirrel is in the cat Bert seed."

"Cindy," said the teacher, "would you please name ten different kinds of cats?"
"Certainly," said Cindy. "A Siamese and nine Angoras."

SOME CAT-CHY JOKES

What do you call . . .
. . . a kitten that makes things happen? *A catalyst.*
. . . a puss that doesn't? *Catatonic.*
. . . a cat that belonged to General Charles Gordon? *Cathoum.*
. . . a feline that can see into the future? *Categ-orical.*
. . . a fur ball that has many sides? *A cathedral.*
. . . a whisker-licker that wakes and goes looking for something to put on fries? *Catsup.*

Q: What's the difference between a kitty that rides behind you in the car, and former Attorney General Katzenbach?
A: Nothing.

"I'm so glad we named the cat Pippin," said Leslie.

"Why?" her mother asked.

"Because that's what everybody calls her!"

"It was sad," the stage manager said to the lighting director. "The house cat was chasing a mouse under the proscenium and *snap*! One of the floorboards gave way and she fell into the basement. Broke all four legs, she did."

"Well," said the lighting director, "at least she didn't fall from the rafters."

"True," said the manager. "I keep telling myself, 'Thank God it's only a stage she was going through.' "

Q: What do you call the loser in a hissing, scratching cat fight?

A: Claude.

"My wife just bought the most beautiful West Indian cat," Fess said to his friend.

"Jamaica?"

"No—she wanted to buy it."

Q: What has claws, a tail, and sees just as well from both ends?

A: A cat with its eyes shut.

Q: What do cats like to eat on a hot day?

A: Mice cream.

The woman walked into the pet store. "I haven't got much money," she told the clerk, "so I'd like to know if you've any kittens you'll let go cheap."

"I'd let them, ma'am," said the clerk, "but they prefer to go meow."

Then there was the man who saw a sign on the pet store that said FREE CATS. So he went in and did.

The police ran up to a woman in the park. "We're looking for a grizzled man with a cat."

"I see," she said. "But wouldn't a blood-hound be more effective?"

The cat had come in from the backyard and was scratching itself furiously. Mrs. Dibney asked her daughter, "Why is the cat *doing* that, honey?"

"Because, Mom, no one else knows where it itches!"

"Does the cat drink milk with a saucer or cup?" the baby-sitter asked Kate.

"Neither," Kate answered. "It uses its tongue."

Bill's mother-in-law came to visit. As soon as she sat down, the cat jumped in her lap and began swiping at the woman's hands.

"Those claws are making my fingers smart!" she complained.

"Quick," cried Bill. "Put her on your head!"

Q: Why are cats such bad dancers?
A: Because they have two left feet.

Holly screamed into the phone, "Doctor, I woke up this morning and my cat was *blue*! What should I do?"

"Cheer it up," the vet suggested.

The teacher asked, "What kind of cats do you find in the tropics?"

Marlene answered, "Hot ones?"

"Ms. Tendler," said the doctor, "I believe your cat has acute thrombosis."

"Thank you," she said, "but what's *wrong* with him?"

Mrs. Idlewild saw Mrs. Kennedy shaking her cat vigorously up and down and to the sides.

"I thought the cat was sick," Mrs. Idlewild said.

"It is."

"Then why on earth are you doing that?"

"I just gave her some medicine," said Mrs. Kennedy, "but I forgot to shake it."

Old Mr. Biddle said to his son, "The cat fell yesterday and was out for four hours."

"How terrible!" said his son. "Where did it fall?"

Mr. Biddle said, "Asleep."

The first grade teacher said, "Clay, can you spell *nice kitty*?"

He thought for a moment, then said, "N-c-e-k-t-t-y."

"You forgot the *i*'s."

"No, I didn't," the boy replied. "They're on the kitty."

The Latin teacher pointed to a picture and said, "Class—can anyone tell me why we call this animal a *cat*?"

Alexander answered, "Because it looks like one, sir?"

Q: What do you call a cat that leads a gang of neutered kitties?
A: Queen of spayeds.

Then there was the cat who swallowed a ball of wool and had mittens.

Old man Perel was walking through the park, his black cat in his arms, when octogenarian Amos shuffled over. Amos stopped short and grinned.

"David Perel, right?"

"Yes?"

"I thought so! It's me . . . *Amos*! It's good to see you after all these years! And your cat—it's grown so! Snowy used to be so small, with long white fur and a cute pink nose."

"Amos, that was fifteen years ago. This is my cat Stormy."

"Incredible," said Amos. "You even changed its name!"

"Logan," said Lois, "does your cat like hair balls?"

"Don't know," said Logan, "he's never been to any."

Abigail said to her rancher father, "I'm going to milk the cat."

Her father shot her a curious look. "How do you intend to do that?"

She replied, "The same way I watered the horse, of course!"

Wendy said to her neighbor, "I heard your cat mewing a six-thirty today."

"I know, and I'm sorry. But my son beats it up every morning."

Wendy gasped. "How awful!"

"What can I do? I just can't get the boy to stay in bed past six."

Q: What do you call a cat that meows all night and loses its voice?
A: Mewtilated.

The vet told a new patient that she had a simple way of remembering every pet's name: She thought of a word that rhymed with the name, then associated that word with that animal.

"So whenever you bring in your cat Wookie," she said, "I shall think of 'Cookie' and remember his name."

Six months later, the patient returned and the vet greeted them.

"And how is little Florio?" she asked.

Q: What's the difference between a dead bee and a mangy cat?
A: One's a bee deceased, the other a seedy beast.

The man was eating a hotdog as he waited for a train. A woman sat down next to him, holding a cat. The feline eyed the hotdog greedily.

"Madam," said the man, "would you mind if I tossed your cat a bit?"

"Not at all," she said with a smile.

The man gently took the cat in his hands and heaved it onto the tracks.

Fortunately, the poor feline was able to get back to its master. It booked passage on the cat-tle car.

The insurance agent said to Mrs. Landwehr, "I've looked over your previous policy, and—tell me. What do you think you'd get if your husband died?"

The woman thought for a moment, then said, "A cat."

Libby was a cross little girl, with a serious problem: Whenever she became upset, she swore. The school psychologist told her parents that a pet might cure her, so they got her a cat.

The instant the kitten entered the house, Libby became a kinder, gentler soul. She would let it go outside, wait by the door, and carry it around with her when it was inside.

On one such jaunt the cat got pregnant, though no one knew it because the animal was always bundled in Libby's arms.

Two months later, the psychologist stopped by the house to see how Libby was doing.

"Fine," her mother said. "She hasn't uttered a single oath."

Just then, the girl's voice rang out from the next room.

"Holy Christ! Shit, man! Screwing hell! The goddam cat's falling apart!"

Q: What kind of cats have their eyes closest together?
A: The smallest ones.

Q: When is a cat like a teenager?
A: When it's between a girl and a woman.

The man noticed a sign on the street that said KITTENS: $3 EACH. Thinking to buy one for his daughter, he went to the door and rang the bell.

An old woman answered, and the man said, "I'd like to buy a kitten. Are they healthy?"

"Oh, yes."

"I see," said the man. "Did you raise them?"

"As a matter of fact I did," she replied. "Yesterday they were $2.50."

Q: What did the house cats do during the blackout?
A: They turned on the mice.

Q: Why are mice like hay?
A: Because the cat'll eat it.

Then there were the two rival cats who went up a tree and had a falling out . . .

. . . and the fancier of Turkish cats who referred to Turkey as his favorite furrin' country.

Miller was visiting with his friend Johnson when a sudden snowstorm began dumping foot after foot of snow.

"You'd better stay the night," Johnson said.

"Yes, perhaps I'd better," Miller said, and went to the closet and put on his coat.

"Where are you going?"
"To get my cat. I don't want to leave her home alone."

Little Audrey said to her schoolmate, "My cat fell off a hundred-foot-tall tree."
"Heavens! Was she hurt?"
"No," Audrey replied. "She was on the bottom."

Q: Where can you learn about biblical kittens?
A: Catechism class.

The teacher said, "If there were ten cats eating in an alley, and another ten cats joined them, how many would that be?"
Henry said, "Twenty-eight."
"Incorrect," said the teacher. "That answer is eight too much."
Henry said, "Did you wanna know how many there were, or what they did?"

Q: When is it truly bad luck to have a black cat cross your path?
A: When you're a mouse.

The baby-sitter asked Marc, "How do you keep the new kitty from sleeping in your bed with you?"
Marc said, "I do what I have to if puss comes, to shove."

Mr. Dugan hollered at his son, "I'll teach you to swing the cat by its tail!"

"That's okay," cried the boy, "I already know how!"

Mrs. Mitchell said to her daughter, "Margaret, you may not have a cat—and that's the *last time* I'll tell you that!"

Margaret smiled. "I just *knew* you'd give in!"

Q: When is a kitten like a teapot?
A: When you're teasin' it.

Q: What sound do Greek cats make?
A: Mu.

Q: How would you describe a cat that wails like Caruso?
A: Mewsical.

Joan said to Ike, "My cat's a mommy!"

"But I thought you had her fixed."

"We did," said Joan. "But she still brought up a hair ball."

Sandy said to a friend, "Last night, my cat was near an American president."

"How?"

"She got a mote in her eye, and sat around a blinkin'."

Arnie woke up and as he went outside to get the newspaper, his cat jumped from the bushes and rushed to his side. Arnie looked down and, much to his chagrin, noticed that someone had painted the cat blue.

With the frightened animal cradled in his arms, Arnie looked around. He noticed a can of blue paint by the new neighbor's garage and stalked over. Arnie pounded on the door.

"Hey!" he screamed. "Did someone inside there paint my cat blue?"

The door opened slowly and a man appeared. He was nearly the size of the door itself, with arms like telephone poles and an expression dark as a thunder-cloud.

"Yeah," said the bruiser. "I did."

Arnie smiled. "I just wanted you to know the first coat's dry."

The two delinquents met in an alley one evening. One of them had a cat tucked under his arm.

"Whatcha got a cat for?" asked the other.

"I ain't got a watch, so I use it to tell time."

"Yeah? How do you do that?"

The kid squeezed the cat until it shrieked. Suddenly someone yelled from an adjoining window, "Will you shut that cat up? It's one o'clock in the morning!"

DOGS

One mail carrier met another at the diner.

"Darn the Woggins dog," said one. "He bit my leg again this morning."

"Did you put anything on it?"

"Naw," said the carrier. "He likes it plain."

Q: What's the quickest way to reach a police dog?
A: Dial K911.

Mrs. Olsen called Mr. Pica, who was the small town's sheriff and dog catcher.

"How quickly can you get here?" she demanded.

"What do you need me for?" he asked. "Dog catching or upholding the law?"

"Both!" she said. "My Pit Bull ran off with a robber in his mouth!"

Then there was the watchdog who never failed to wake his master whenever there was a burglar in the house. He did it by crawling under the bed.

Even worse was the watchdog who barked so loud his owners never heard the robbers coming or going.

Q: What does a Chow Chow say when you turn it inside out?
A: Ouch ouch!

The teacher asked little Linda, "Can you tell me if a dog has more of a covering on its body in the summer or in the winter?"
Linda thought for a moment then said, "In the summer."
The teacher asked, "Why do you say that?"
Linda replied, " 'Cause in the winter it wears a coat, but in the summer it wears a coat *and* pants."

Little Linda had another unusual notion about dogs, that they were bigger in the evening than in the morning.
When a classmate told her to prove it, Linda replied, "Isn't *every* dog let out at night and taken in the next day?"

Q: What's the difference between a mad dog and a hotdog?
A: One bites the hands that feeds it, the other feeds the hand that bites it.

Four-year-old Zach was terrified of dogs. Hoping to cure him of his fear, his mother took his hand and walked him over to a neighbor, who owned a gentle old Saint Bernard. They approached the animal, who was lying on the stoop.

"Hold out your hand," Zach's mother said softly.

Reluctantly, the boy did as he was told. The dog looked up with sad eyes, raised its head, then slowly dragged its big tongue across Zach's hand.

"There," the woman said. "That wasn't so bad, was it?"

"Not yet," Zach replied.

"What do you mean, not yet?"

"That was just a taste while he decides if he wants to eat me!"

Later, Zach and his mother passed another dog. It ran over to them, yipping and wagging its tail. Zach leapt into his mother's arms.

"Don't worry," said his mother. "Look how happy she is to see you."

Zach glanced down at the dog and asked, "How do you know which end to believe?"

Q: What does the dog warden give to dogs that just won't shut up?
A: Barking tickets.

Stupid Steve said to Smart Sally, "I don't get it! How come you were able to teach your dog all kinds of neat tricks, but I can't teach mine *nothing*?"

"It's easy," said Sally, "but first you've got to know more than the dog."

Steve's dog was loyal, though. It accompanied its master to school each and every day. This continued until the dog graduated and they had to part.

Q: How did the dumb dog get a bloody forehead?
A: From chasing parked cars.

Daniel walked over to his neighbor. "Say—did you know your dog bit my wife yesterday?"

"No, but I suppose you're going to sue me for damages."

"Not at all," said Daniel. "What do you want for the dog?"

What do you call a dog with . . .
. . . a cold? *A Germy Shepherd*.
. . . a nasty temper? *A Wire Fox Terror*.
. . . a great sense of humor? *A Chihuahahaha*.
. . . a bad voice? *A Joe Cocker Spaniel*.
. . . a really good voice? *A Buddy Collie*.
. . . a bad voice *and* no more career? *A Mastiffany*.
. . . a fondness for bowling? *A Doberman Tenpinscher*.
. . . a mean guitar? *A Bassist Hound*.
. . . a wicked growl? *A Grrrrrreat Dane*.

. . . a degree in chemistry? *A Laboratory Retriever.*

. . . a great sense of humor? *A Joke Russell Terrier.*

. . . a big family? *Lotsa Apsos.*

. . . ticks? *A watchdog.*

Ed was going to be late for the regular Friday night card game. Rather than cancel, the host suggested that his dog could play the fourth hand until Ed arrived.

The others were dubious, but they wanted to play and gave the dog a chance. To their surprise, the dog was a heckuva player.

When Ed finally arrived, he watched with amazement as the dog won a small pot, and then another. Taking his seat after the dog left, Ed said, "Wow—that was incredible! A dog playing poker!"

"Not so incredible," one of the men snorted. "Every time he got a good hand, he wagged his tail."

After being chased from the apple orchard by a fierce Doberman, Pete rubbed his sore derriere and said to his friend, "A dog's bark may be worse than its bite, but I prefer the bark."

Q: What kind of bark tells you *instantly* to Beware of the Dog?
A: A tree with a sign on it.

Mrs. Flynn took Nancy aside after class.

"Young lady, this essay about your dog is the same one your brother handed in last year, word for word. What do you have to say about that?"

Nancy shrugged. "Same dog."

Q: What's Lassie's favorite food?
A: Collie flour.

Philpott took his dog to the vet. "Dr. Scott, I want you to cut off his tail."

The vet was horrified. "Why on earth should I do that?"

"Because my mother-in-law's coming, and I don't want *anything* to make her think she's welcome."

Then there was the veterinarian who worked on a dog by the seat of his pants: He examined the hound's lungs . . .

. . . and the Great Dane who was a terrific watchdog. He watched robbers take the VCR, the TV, the computer, the CD player . . .

. . . and the two whacko dogs who got their own TV series. The title? Twin Pekes.

Q: What does a ship's mast have in common with a young dog in a refrigerator?
A: One's perpendicular, the other's pup in de cooler.

Nikolai walked into the Leningrad apartment of his sister Valya. Much to his surprise, their pet Chihuahua had been replaced by the largest Weimaraner he'd ever seen.

"Valya, you've got twelve children in a one-room apartment! Why did you get such a big animal?"

"*Kapusta!*" Valya said. "It keeps them from arguing."

"Because they're afraid of him?"

"*Nyet!* Now everyone can pet him at once!"

Valya liked the dog too, and because it was so handsome she decided to enter it in a dog show. When she came home wearing a dour expression, her husband Piotr asked, "How did you do?"

"I won first prize."

"Splendid! Then why do you look so sad?"

Valya sighed. "I wanted the dog to win."

Then there was misanthropic Benson, whose dog became rabid and bit him.

After examining him in the hospital emergency room, the doctor said, "I'm afraid you've contracted rabies."

The man nodded gravely and, grabbing the doctor's pen and prescription pad, began writing furiously.

"Look," said the doctor, "hydrophobia is serious, but there's no need to write a will!"

"Oh, this isn't a will," Benson replied. "It's the people I want to bite."

Q: Why does a Dalmation have such a difficult time hiding?
A: Because it's always spotted.

Nanook the Eskimo was hauled into court for bigamy.

"You had wives in Juneau, Nome, Anchorage, and Fairbanks," said the judge. "How could you *do* that?"

Nanook answered, "Hardy sled dogs."

Avon lady Isabel entered the house cautiously, for there as a Great Dane snarling behind its master.

"Oh, don't be such a 'fraidy cat!" the owner said. "This pooch'll eat off your hand."

Isabel replied, "That's what I'm afraid of."

Q: Why is a limping dog like a hill?
A: One's a slow pup, the other a slope up.

It was a most unusual advertisement: The obedience school not only promised to train your dog in a week, but to teach it a foreign language.

Though dubious, Ms. Stevens dropped off her dog Uther and, a week later, returned to pick it up.

While they were driving home, the woman was impressed at how well behaved the dog was. Still she felt rather foolish as she asked, "So tell me, Uth—did you really learn a foreign language?"

The dog looked up and replied, "Meow."

Q: What's the difference between a dog and a member of Greenpeace?
A: One's a tail wagger, the other a whale tagger.

Then there was the dog who went into its owner's study, hopped on the desk, and began chewing on the dictionary. Fortunately, the owner caught the animal in the act and took the words right out of its mouth.

While browsing through her records, the dog warden noticed that Mr. Kahrs had forgotten to renew his dog license.
Driving out to the house, the warden said, "Mr. Kahrs, are you aware that your dog license expired on the twelfth?"
"I know," he said. "And are you aware the dog did too?"

Q: What do Pinocchio and a little boy's newborn dog have in common?
A: One's a puppet, the other a pup-pet.

Five-year-old Dom said to his little neighbor Rita, "Wanna come over and see my dog?"
"I didn't know you had a dog," said Rita.
"Yeah—just got her."
"Does she bite?"

Dom replied, "That's what I want to find out."

Q: What do you call a hunter who accidentally shoots his pointer?
A: Disappointed.

Mrs. Merritt yelled to her son, "Kyle! Will you keep that dog *out* of the house? It's full of fleas!"

Kyle turned to the mutt beside him. "Sorry, Jake, but you can't come in the house. It's full of fleas."

Then there was the dog who visited a flea circus and stole the show . . .

. . . and another dog who started a flea circus from scratch.

Q: What's the difference between a Rodin statue and a hungry dog?
A: One's a Thinker, the other a thin cur.

Young Sharon walked up to her music teacher.

"I got a new dog," she said, "and I wanted to name it Sousa, after the composer."

"What a nice thought!" said the teacher.

"Yes, but my mother wouldn't let me. She said it would be an insult to Mr. Sousa. So I said I wanted to name it after you—but my mother wouldn't let me do that either."

"I can understand that," said the teacher.

"Yes. She told me it would be an insult to the dog."

Then there was the dog who was sauntering down the street when he saw a bench with a sign that said WET PAINT. He gladly obliged.

Sam was sitting in the barber's chair when he noticed the owner's dog staring at him.

"The dog seems fascinated by what you're doing," Sam observed. "He's watching your every more."

"Oh, he couldn't care less about hair," said the barber.

"Then why's he staring?"

"Because sometimes I snip off an ear."

Q: What's the difference between a high-class dog and one that never argues with you?

A: One's a pedigree, the other pet agrees.

Shackleton and his beloved husky Kai were stranded on an ice floe near the North Pole. Days passed, and hunger finally got the better of the adventurer: Building a fire, he reluctantly ate the dog.

After finishing his meal, Shackleton looked wistfully at the dog's remains.

"Poor Kai," he sighed. "How he would've *loved* those bones."

Q: What do you find on the ground when it rains cats and dogs?
A: Lots of poodles.

Then there was the Arctic explorer who said that the honor of reaching the top of the world really belonged to his dogs.

"They were the ones who got to the pole first."

Q: What's the difference between a mean French dog and a piece of ziti?
A: One's a nasty poodle, the other a pasta noodle.

The Dachshund was curled up and snoozing on the front lawn when all of a sudden it opened its eyes and gazed upon the cutest little dog it had ever seen.

"I think I love you," the Dachshund said impulsively.

"Don't be a jerk," replied the vision. "I'm your backside."

Hear about the boastful sheepdog who ran up to the hard-of-hearing one in the meadow?

"I herd ewes!" boasted the hardworking sheepdog.

The other looked at him and replied, "I'm sorry, but I didn't say anything."

Q: Why do dogs run so quickly in the western plains?
A: It's a long way between trees.

Sue was walking her well-groomed poodle down the street.

"Gracious," said her friend Tony, "her tail's so fluffy, how do you tell the head and tail apart?"

"Simple," said Sue. "I give a little tug, and if it bites it's the head."

Q: How do you spell dog backward?
A: D-o-g-b-a-c-k-w-a-r-d.

Will brought his pet dog and pet canary to the Las Vegas talent agent. The agent watched with disinterest as the bird drank from a cup of water and the dog did a handstand. He was about to throw Will and his pets out when the dog suddenly cleared its throat and said, "Thank you for watching, sir. I hope you'll hire us!"

The agent shot to his feet. "That's amazing! The dog's hired!"

"Just the dog? Not the bird?"

"Just the dog," said the agent.

The next day, the hound made his debut at one of the hottest nightclubs in town. The animal hopped around on its front paws for a minute, then cleared its throat and walked offstage.

The agent looked on with horror. "Hey, what's *wrong*? Why didn't it *talk*?"

"Talk? Sir, that dog can't talk."

"But yesterday, in my office—"

Will looked pained. "I tried to tell you, sir."

"Tell me *what*?"

"About the *bird*. She's a ventriloquist."

Q: How do you stop a Pit Bull from charging?
A: Take away its credit cards.

City boy Ernie went to visit his friend Tom in the country.

"You look pale," Tom said. "You need some sun. Why don't you take my rifle and my two retrievers and do some hunting?"

Ernie had never hunted before, but decided to do as his friend suggested. Fifteen minutes later, he was back.

"That was *fun!*" Ernie gushed.

"So why'd you come back?"

"I need more dogs to hunt," Ernie said.

As he was leaving for work, Allan walked over to his neighbor Wilson.

"I'm getting a little concerned here," Allan said. "Did you know your dog barked *all night*?"

"I wouldn't worry about it," Wilson said. "He gets his sleep during the day."

Q: What do you call a dog that wears designer clothes?
A: Bill Blassie.

What do you get when you cross . . .
. . . a Dachshund with a Pointer? *A doctor.*
. . . a Maltese with a Samoyed? *A malted.*
. . . a Basset Hound with a Corgi? *A baggy.*
. . . a Beagle with a Retriever? *A beaver.*
. . . a Newfie with a Poodle? *A noodle.*

Q: What do you get when you cross a dog and a lion?
A: A very anxious mail carrier.

Q: What game do members of the K9 Corps really enjoy?
A: Dog tag.

Then there was the veterinarian who spayed dogs for free. As he promised in his advertisements, "Come in to avoid those pregnant paws . . ."

. . . . and the pet store which sold a litter of Dachshunds by advertising, "Get a long, little doggie . . ."

. . . and the super-wealthy oil sheik who bought his dog a boy.

Q: Why do dogs chase their tails?
A: They're trying to make ends meet.

Q: What does a dog with a sore throat say?
A: Bow-*owww*!

Shay came home crying.

"Where's your dog?" her mother asked.

"Kai ran away," Shay said, sobbing, "and I've looked *everywhere* for her!"

"Don't worry," her mother said, wiping away her tears. "We'll put a lost and found ad in the paper."

"That won't help!" the girl bawled. "Kai can't *read*!"

Q: What's the difference between a sultry time of summer and actress Doris's pet?
A: One's Dog Days, the other's Day's dog.

What do you call . . .

. . . the shortcut that sea dogs take through Central America? *The Panama Kennel.*

. . . a dog that's lefthanded? *A southpaw.*

. . . a contrary German shepherd? *A K-nein.*

. . . a mongrel that's been run over by a truck? *Dog tired.*

. . . an all-dog heavy metal band? *Muttallica.*

. . . a dog who loves the Big Apple? *A New Yorkie.*

. . . a dog owned by Dracula? *A bloodhound.*

. . . the place where Millie Bush likes to take her vacations? *Kennelbunkport, Maine.*

. . . dogs migrating out West? *A Waggin'* *train.*

Q: What's the difference between Benji and Sirius?
A: Nothing! They're both dog stars.

Q: What's the difference between a little girl who likes a little boy, and a little girl who likes a little dog?
A: Nothing again! Both are puppy love.

Marta's old dog died and she bought a new one. Because the pup was so full of energy, she called him Life. Unfortunately, Marta used her old dog's things on the new one, and while she was out walking the puppy, its frayed leather strap snapped and it ran away, never to return.

Moral: It pays to get a new leash on Life.

Q: What toast did Mr. Wickfield offer when he found Mr. Heep hiding with his scruffy hound?
A: "Here's mutt an' Uriah."

Orlito came home and found his wife crying. Ignoring the smell of burned food and smoke so common to their kitchen, he said, "What's the matter, honey?"

The woman looked at her husband through bloodshot eyes. "The dog ate the cake I baked for your birthday."

"That's okay," Orlito said. "I'll buy you a new dog."

Q: What's the difference between an extremely dumb dog and an extremely dumb medical student?
A: None. You can't teach either to heel.

Q: What's the difference between a mangy dog and a cowardly one?
A: One has fleas, the other flees.

Then there was the blind man who walked into a bookstore, got a tight grip on the leash of his Seeing Eye dog, and began swinging him around and around his head.

Horrified, the clerk rushed over. "Sir, can I help you?"

"Nope," said the blind man. "Just browsing."

Q: What did the man say when he came home and found his Terrier missing?
A: "Doggone!"

Then there was the dog gunslinger who walked into the tavern and placed his bandaged forearm on the bar.

"What can I do for you?" the bartender said warily.

Holding the man in his steely gaze, the animal said, "I'm lookin' for the man who shot my paw."

Q: What's the best way to describe *Canterbury Tails*?
A: Litterature.

Q: What's the difference between a church which follows a specific system of principles, and an orphaned pup?
A: One's got dogma, the other doesn't.

Q: What's the difference between a sick dog and one that won't stop barking?
A: One feels awful, the other feels arf-full.

Sir Canhead was out riding on a blizzard-stricken day when his horse died. Struggling through the snow, the knight came upon a huge sheepdog. Because he was exhausted, Canhead threw himself on the animal's back. The dog gamely carried the knight to the nearest inn, where the noble warrior rapped weakly on the door.

When the innkeeper opened the door, the knight gasped, "Good sir! Perchance, would you have a room?"

"Sorry," said the man, "the archery tournament's in town—all the rooms are taken."

The knight wheezed, "Then . . . might I just sit by your fire and warm myself?"

"But of course," said the proprietor, glancing at the sheepdog as he helped the man in. "I would never let a knight out on a dog like this."

When the puppy chewed a big hole in the carpet, Mrs. Burk told her son the dog had to go.

"No!" the boy cried. "I'll train him, I promise!"

His mother shook her head. "I'm afraid it's too late for that. Once they get a habit like this, it can't be broken."

"No, Mom, I *can* train him. I'll teach him to lie on the hole and he *won't budge!*"

Mrs. Michaelson went to a movie theater showing a revival of *Wuthering Heights*. Shortly after Heathcliff's disappearance, she heard sobbing several rows behind her. Turning, she saw a Welsh Corgi sitting beside its master, using its tiny paw to wipe a tear from its eye.

The dog wept even more when Catherine died, and when the picture was over Mrs. Michaelson went to the owner.

"I can't believe that dog of yours was so moved by the film!"

"Me neither," said the man. "He absolutely *hated* the book."

The man and his dog went to another movie. Standing in the back of the theater, an usher watched as the dog ate a bucket of popcorn before the movie started.

Unable to control himself, the usher walked over to the man.

"Sir, I just watched your dog eat a bucket

of popcorn, and I've gotta tell you—that's the craziest thing I ever saw."

"I know," said the man. "Milk Duds are so much better."

The man and his dog went to a rock concert, only this time the woman in the box office wouldn't sell them a ticket.

"Sorry," she said. "No dogs allowed in here."

The man refused to accept that and, running to a nearby drugstore, he bought sunglasses and a cane, then went back to the box office.

"Sorry," the woman said. "You can't bring the dog in."

"But it's a Seeing Eye dog!"

"Really? Seeing Eye dogs are supposed to be German Shepherds."

Thinking quickly, the man recoiled and blurted, "You mean . . . he's *not*?"

The man finally got into the concert by hiding the dog under his coat. A security guard noticed the bulge in the coat and, thinking he was smuggling in booze, walked over. He gave the bulge a whack with his billy club and, sure enough, something came trickling out the bottom of the man's coat.

Catching some in his hand and tasting it, the guard crowed, "Aha! Scotch!"

"No," the man corrected. "Welsh."

Q: What does a dog do that a person steps in?

A: Pants.

Goldstein walked into the office of the theatrical producer and set a little dog on his desk.

"Sir," said Goldstein, "this little dog wants to play Hamlet on Broadway. Can you help him?"

Puffing on his cigar, the producer decided to humor the man. "Sure," he said. "Let me hear him say a few lines."

Standing on his little hind legs, the dog cleared his throat and said, "There are more things in heaven and earth, than are dreamt of in your—"

Suddenly the office door flew open and a large dog stalked over. She grabbed the little dog by its paw, yanked it around, and vanished into the hallway.

"Who was *that*?" the agent asked.

Goldstein sighed. "His mother. She wants him to be a doctor."

Colon walked into a bar with his mutt. After ordering a beer for himself and a Shirley Temple for the dog, Colon said to the bartender, "I'll bet you a C note my dog can talk."

"You're on," said the bartender. He removed two fifties from the cash register and slapped them on the bar.

Colon pulled five twenties from his wallet and placed them beside the fifties. He turned to his dog and asked, "How would you describe sandpaper?"

"Ruff."

"On what part of a house will you find an aerial?"

The dog answered, "Ruff."

"Who was the greatest baseball player who ever lived?"

The dog said, "Ruff."

"Wait a minute," the bartender said. "What do you think I am, stupid?"

The dog looked at him. "Okay—maybe it was Aaron."

Colon's sister Maria also had a run-in with a talking dog on the streets of New York. As she walked to work, a Cocker Spaniel walked up to her, tugged on her skirt, and asked, "Can you tell me how to get to Madison Avenue?"

Maria looked down at the dog. "I must be imagining things. Y-you can *talk*?"

"Of course," said the dog.

Bundling the animal in her arms, she raced to her office, plopped the animal on her desk, and announced to everyone in the pool, "I'll bet everyone here a dollar that this dog can talk!"

Twenty people came over and slapped down dollar bills. Smiling at the dog, Maria said, "Okay—do that again."

The dog cocked its head to one side and stared dumbly up at her, panting.

"Talk!" she said.

The dog continued to stare.

Her coworkers laughed. After Maria had paid them all off and they'd returned to their desks, she sat down and glowered at the animal. "I *knew* I only imagined that you talked."

"Nonsense," whispered the dog. "Think of the odds we'll get at lunchtime."

Q: How do you cure fleas on a dog?
A: Depends on what's wrong with them.

After hearing a shot, farmer Jones ran to the farm of his neighbor, Smith. He found Smith sitting outside the barn, weeping, a smoking shotgun across his lap.

"What happened?" Jones asked.

Through his tears, Smith replied, "I—I had to shoot my dog."

"Good lord! Was he mad?"

"Well," said Smith, "he wasn't exactly *overjoyed*."

Then there were the two country dogs who were visiting the city. While finishing up at the fire hydrant, one happened to glance down the street at the parking meters.

"Whaddya know?" he said. "Pay toilets."

Q: What's the difference between a dirty dog and a dead yellowjacket?
A: One's a seedy beast, the other a bee deceased.

Walking down the street with his powerful Pit Bull, McGuirk laughed when he saw Dweeble approaching with a big but gangly mutt. The animal had a sloped back and a long, drooping tail.

"Pretty sorry-looking pooch you got there," McGuirk said. "You oughta get a tough dog like mine."

"Oh, my pet isn't so sorry," replied Dweeble. "In fact, he's tough enough to lick your dog in a fight."

"But my dog's a prizewinner."

"I still think he could take him."

McGuirk stiffened and let his Pit Bull loose on Dweeble's animal.

Dweeble's pet was unfazed. He grabbed the Pit Bull's head in his teeth, picked him up, and spit him across the street.

McGuirk was aghast. "You weren't kidding about your dog being tough. Where on earth did you get him?"

"Africa." Dweeble smiled. "Though I *did* cut off the mane to keep the fleas away."

Smedley was walking through the mall when he noticed a dog in the pet shop window. The animal was on its knees, its hands folded in prayer, its lips moving. The sign on the cage read MARKED DOWN TO $5.

Smedley walked in and stood before the cage.

"Please buy me," the dog implored. "I *hate* being here. I'm really a very special dog. I've traveled in space, I've climbed K2, I've gone pearl diving, and I even competed in the Olympics."

Smedley hurried over to the owner. "That dog in the window—it *talks*!"

"Sure does," says the owner.

"Then why are you selling him . . . and so cheap?"

The man replied, "I just *won't* have a liar in my shop!"

Q: What's the difference between buying a well-trained dog and a big, destructive one?
A: One comes housebroken, the other leaves your house broken.

Mrs. Standish was complaining to Mrs. Miles about her teenage son.

"He's so lazy, it's impossible to get him out of bed in the morning."

"You ought to do what I do," said Mrs. Miles. "I just let the dog in his room."

"That wakes him up?"

"You bet it does. He sleeps with the cat."

Q: What did Nick Charles call his dancing dog?

A: Fred Asta.

Q: What happened to the dog that swallowed a firefly?

A: It barked with delight.

The old dog was wheezing horribly as Bernie took him for a walk.

"Say," said a passerby, "that dog oughta be checked."

"Why?" said Bernie. "I *like* him black."

"Suppose you had four puppies," Erica said to Gregory, "and I asked you for one. How many would you have left?"

Gregory answered without hesitation, "Four."

Q: What do you call a fox being chased by dogs?

A: Hounded.

Q: How would you describe the hounds that are chasing the fox?

A: Dogged.

Drummond had owned Poochly for ten years, and for ten years the dog would wake up, walk over to its food dish, and wait patiently for its owner to come and feed it.

One day Drummond overslept. The dog sat

and sat and finally went to the bedroom. Poochly put its paws beside its sleeping master and said, "Excuse me, but it's nearly eleven o'clock and I'm *starved!*"

Drummond was suddenly wide awake. "Poochly! Y-you can *talk*!"

"Yes."

"Then why haven't you said anything for a decade?"

The dog replied, "Up till now, the service has been excellent."

Q: What do you get from owning a pet dog and a pet chicken?
A: Barkin' and eggs.

Millicent asked the vet, "Is it true that a mad dog won't attack you if you carry garlic?"

"That depends," replied the vet, "on how fast you carry it."

Q: What's the difference between baseball cards and rabid dogs?
A: You wouldn't mind tearing into a pack of baseball cards.

Q: How do you turn a mad dog into an oath?
A: Turn it around.

The man stormed into the pet shop and dropped the Jack Russell Terrier on the counter.

"You said this dog is good for cats, but all it does is lay on the floor!"

"So?" said the owner. "Isn't that good for cats?"

Q: What do you get when you cross a dog with a fish?

A: I don't know, but it's great at chasing submarines.

Winston was drafted, so he gave his ditzy fiancée Rachel a dog.

"Whenever you look at him, you'll think of me," Winston said.

Rachel stared at the dog for a long time, then said, "But Win . . . he doesn't look a thing like you."

Mrs. Berkow entered her mutt Mitzi in a dog show.

"You really think you've got a chance of winning?" one of the judges asked.

"Not at all," said Mrs. Berkow. "But I'm hoping my Mitzi will meet some nice dogs."

Marie said to her husband Antoine, "Poor Renfrew's hearing isn't what it used to be."

"Rubbish," he said. "Watch this. Renny, come. Now roll over. Sit."

Marie glanced down. "Now, Antoine—*you* clean it up."

Xavier lost his treasured pet poodle and placed an ad in the paper, offering a $5,000 reward to anyone who found the dog. The next day, he returned to the newspaper office to see if there'd been any response to the ad. Much to his surprise, no one was there except for the receptionist.

"Where is everyone?" he asked.

"Out looking for your dumb dog," was her reply.

Minnie said to her neighbor Marge, "Our dog is just like a member of the family."

"Which one?" Marge asked.

Q: What position did the dog play on the football team?

A: Arfback.

Then there was the dummy who didn't bother to get his dog license, since the animal wasn't going to do any driving.

"Sheesh!" Dinsdale said to his friend. "Did my dog get in hot water last night!"

"Why, what'd he do?"

Dinsdale replied, "Took a bath, he did."

"Does your dog have fleas?" Pepe asked Juanita.

"No," said Juanita. "She has puppies."

Werner walked into a pet shop. "Do you carry dogs?"

The owner said, "Only if they aren't too heavy."

Q: What's the difference between buying a puppy and getting it home?
A: In the pet shop, you choose the pup; at home, it's the pup that chews.

Acta, the stunt dog, was about to jump into a lake from a fifty-foot-high cliff when his trainer shouted for him to stay put.

"What's wrong?" screamed the director.

"Are you crazy?" the trainer yelled back. "There're only six inches of water in that lake!"

"Of course," said the director. "You think I want your dog to drown?"

The agent called the aspiring novelist. "You know that manuscript you sent me? Well, there's good news and bad news."

"Really?"

"Yes. The good news is that Signet ate it up."

"No kidding! So . . . what's the bad news?"

"Signet's my dog."

Q: What do you call it when a dog talks to itself?
A: Muttering.

The spinster Edna never left the house, and she had a dog that she also never let out of the house. One day Edna's sister Alma convinced her to take a cruise. Edna reluctantly agreed, under the condition that Alma come over and feed the dog . . . and never let it out.

After a week, Alma received a postcard from her sister. It read, "Met a lovely man and am having an incredible time. P.S.: Let the dog out!"

Moshe and Harold left six pounds of chopped meat on the kitchen table, then went out to fire up the barbecue. When they came back, the meat was gone and the Cocker Spaniel was sitting in the corner, fat and content.

"I'll bet he ate it!" Moshe roared and, grabbing the animal, carried it to the bathroom and made it sit on the scale. The scale registered eight pounds.

"Hmmm," said Harold. "It couldn'ta been him."

"Why not?"

"What're you, stupid?" Moshe said. "That dog weighs more than two pounds!"

The first grade teacher asked Louis, "What do we call the outside of a tree?"

Louis clearly had no idea, so the girl sitting next to him said from the side of her mouth, "Bark, Louis. Bark."

Louis perked up and said, "Bowwow! Bowwow!"

Dale couldn't understand why he didn't get any takers after putting an ad in the paper for his dog's litter:

FREE GERMAN SHEPHERD PUPPIES. DE-VOTED, PLAYFUL, EAT ANYTHING, ESPE-CIALLY LIKE CHILDREN.

"Mommy," said the girl, "is it true that all living things are made from dust?"

"Yes."

"And that they return to dust when they die?"

"Yes."

"Well, I just looked under the bed, and the dog's either coming or going."

There was a knock on the apartment door. When Ms. Thompson answered, a messenger said, "Here's the muzzle from Rusty's Dog World."

"I didn't order a muzzle."

"I know," said the messenger. "Your neighbors did."

Young Harry walked into the house; he was dirty and covered with scratches, his clothes in tatters.

"What happened?" his father asked.

"I was attacked by the Great Dane down the street."

"Didn't you read that book I gave you, the one that said if you stare straight into a dog's eyes it won't bother you?"

"Sure did," said Harry. "Problem is, the dog didn't read it."

The man was sitting on his front stoop with a beautiful German Shepherd. Nate happened to be passing by and, since he'd been intending to get a watchdog, offered to buy the majestic animal.

"I'll give you five hundred dollars for it," Nate said.

"I don't know," replied the man. "She don't look too good."

"Nonsense, my good man, she looks fine. I promise to treat her well; she'll be a very contented watchdog."

"Really, mister—she don't look well."

"Look," Nate said, "I'll give you seven hundred and fifty."

The man couldn't resist and took the money, handed Nate the leash, then watched the dog stumble off the stoop. It walked into a tree, tripped over a boulder, and finally sat down, refusing to budge.

"Hey," Nate said. "This dog is blind!"

As he counted his money, the man said, "I told you she didn't look too good."

Q: What did the boy shout when his Scottish Terrier fell from the airplane?
A: "The Skye is falling!"

Patrick said to his neighbor, "What was that horrible noise I heard in the middle of the night?"

"It was my sheepdog," said the woman. "He fell down the steps."

"Cellar?"

"No. Who'd buy a dog with four broken legs?"

Q: What's the difference between a large Australian dog and ladies who like to gamble at church?
A: One's a big Dingo, the others dig bingo.

Q: How do all dogs feel when they grow up?
A: Not very whelp.

Farmer Gary asked his hand Nathan, "Do you know why my hound Morty paints his claws green?"

"No, why?"

"So he can hide in the lettuce patch and surprise the rabbits."

"That's ridiculous," Nathan said. "I've never seen Morty in the lettuce patch."

"See?" said Gary. "It works!"

Q: What do you call mad dogs that like to go rafting down the river?
A: Whitewater rabids.

Mrs. Hepburn commissioned a doghouse for her beloved Poopsie. When the carpenter was finished, he proudly showed her his handiwork.

"It's flawless," he boasted.

"Oh, dear," said Mrs. Hepburn. "Then what will my Poopsie walk on?"

"Junior," said Helen, "please give the puppy some peanut butter."

"Peanut butter?"

"Yes. It's good for growing dogs."

"Ohhhh," said Junior, "I always *wondered* where they came from."

Kevin said to Julia, "My dog can pick up a cent with her tongue."

"Big deal," Julia replied. "My dog can do that with his nose."

Trying again to engage the girl in conversation, Kevin said, "My dog sleeps with me every night."

"Mine too."

"Yes, but my dog's a Great Dane. We had to have an extra-big bed built so she could fit."

Julia turned up her nose and replied, "That's a lot of bunk!"

Q: What did the performing dog do when the audience began applauding?
A: He replied with a deep bowwow.

"Mildred," said the teacher, "if you had five dogs and I gave you five more, what would you get?"

The girl thought for a moment, then replied, "A bigger doghouse."

Young Ethel was walking through the park, peering behind bushes.

"What are you looking for?" a police officer asked.

"A dog," she said.

"I see. And where did you lose it?"

Ethel said, "I didn't lose it. I just want one."

Efrem was walking his dog when he stopped at his friend's house.

"Betcha a dollar my dog's the smartest one in the world."

The friend was game, and after they'd both placed a dollar on the ground Efrem said to the dog, "Bang! You're dead!"

The dog just stood there."

"See?" said the friend. "He's not so smart."

"Baloney," said Efrem, scooping up the money. "He knows he's not dead!"

Q: What do you say to a dog before dinner?
A: Bone appetit!

Then there was the man who complained that when it came to walking the dog, his children liked to do nothing better . . .

. . . and the 'fraidy-cat dog who was named Cinderella, because she always ran away from the ball . . .

. . . and the man who was flattered when his date said he reminded her of a championship boxer she once met—at the Westminster Dog Show . . .

. . . and the dyslexic evangelist who commended his neighbor after the fellow put up a sign that said BEWARE OF DOG . . .

. . . and the restaurant which served dogs, and had the slogan "Furs come, furs served . . ."

. . . and Snoopy, who quit his strip because he was tired of working for *Peanuts* . . .

. . . and the pet shop owner who went out of business when she lost her leash.

And where do you think the dogs of that pet shop owner were sent? To the paw house, naturally.

Q: What's the difference between a dog burying a bone and a heckler?
A: Nothing. They both rely on digs to get what they want.

Q: What was the motto of Will Rogers's dog?
A: "I never met a man I didn't lick."

Q: Why did the dog give birth to puppies on the road?
A: Because the sign said FINE FOR LITTERING.

C.B. flunked his dog obedience school test, and his master Jessie was ticked off. Cornering the instructor after class, she said, "I really don't think my dog deserved a zero on that test."

"I agree," said the instructor. "Unfortunately, that's the lowest grade I'm permitted to give."

Q: Which has more legs: no dog, or one dog?
A: No dog. One dog has four legs, but no dog has more.

Q: How did the dog get into the locked house?
A: He kept running around and around until he was all in.

Q: What's the difference between a bee and a bad dog?
A: One gets honey, the other whacks.

Then there was the dog who loved classical music. All he did each day was Bach and Bach.

In fact, the dog Beethoven at the moon . . .

. . . though you could never find him, 'cause he was always Hayden in the bushes.

Q: However, what composer is *the* favorite among dogs?
A: Poochini.

Then there was the vet who was so sick of treating dogs he threw a distemper tantrum . . .

. . . and the vet who opened a pound which he nicknamed his used cur lot.

"My nutty uncle once pulled the tail of a mad dog," Lance said to Joey.

"Wow! What happened?"
"It was the end of him."

One vet said to another, "Did you hear about the new canine scale?"
"No, what about it?"
"It only works in dog pounds."

Q: Why did the dog book passage on the Concorde?
A: Because he was a jet-setter.

Q: What do you get when you cross a pug-faced dog with a hippopotamus?
A: A heavyweight boxer.

The professor at the agricultural college asked his students, "What's the best time to pick apples?"
Hortense answered, "When the neighbor's dog is asleep."

"Son, don't you think you should walk the dog?"
"But Dad—I don't want to!"
"Come, now," said the man, "walking a dog never killed anyone."
"How do you know I won't be the first?" asked the lad.

The groomer walked out to the waiting room. "Ms. Welch, was your poodle wearing a bright red kerchief?"

"No—"

"That's too bad."

"Why?"

"I fear I've cut its throat."

Malvern was upset. After spending a day in the woods with his brand-new Labrador Retriever, he realized that the animal was the worst hunting dog on earth. It couldn't follow a scent, preferred chasing butterflies to heeling, and tired easily.

Driving ninety miles to the nearest town, Malvern went to the library and grabbed a book called *How to Hunt*, hoping that somewhere inside he'd find helpful hints about training a hunting dog.

Settling down by the campfire, Malvern was crushed: He'd grabbed volume eight of the encyclopedia.

Then there was the man who went tramping through the woods with his dog. Of course, the tramps weren't too thrilled.

The mail carrier brought a parcel for Larry. He opened it, removed a collar, then unwrapped a metal tag.

"It's the dog's new license and collar," Larry said to the mail carrier. He turned the two items over in his hand. "Those lazy twits! I suppose I have to put this on myself."

"Actually," said the carrier, "I think you're supposed to put it on the dog."

Q: Where do homeless little puppies go?
A: To the arfanage.

Q: Where do dogs stay when they go camping?
A: In a pup tent.

Then there was the dog that barked because it had fleas. After a few hours, it was both hoarse and buggy . . .

. . . fortunately, while most dogs are washable, they shrink from it.

Q: What kind of cheese do dogs put on pizza?
A: Muttsarella.

Giselle, the maid, had been fired, and as she left the Ballon mansion she threw a handful of dog biscuits to the dog.

"That was very kind of you," said Mr. Ballon.

"It so happens, sir, that I never forget a friend," said Giselle. "That was for helping me clean the dishes all these years."

As the fire truck zoomed past, three children looked with reverence at the majestic Dalmation riding on the hook-and-ladder truck.

"I'll bet they use him to pull kids to safety," said one child.

"Naw," said another. "They use him to keep people away from the fire."

"You're both wrong," said the third.

"Oh?" said the others in unison. "What's he for?"

The child replied, "They use him to find the fire hydrant."

Then there was the world's dumbest dog, who ate a bone, then got up and found that it only had three legs . . .

. . . and the sage who noted that while every dog has its day, only one with a broken tail has its weak end.

Q: What did Dwight Gooden do when the female dog leapt at him on the mound?

A: He pitched a bitch.

After reading Amanda's composition about her dog, the teacher asked, "Don't you know how to spell Chihuahua?"

"Yes," the girl protested. "I just don't know when to stop."

Willie walked into the house all tattered and torn.

"What happened to you?" his mother cried.

"I challenged Mike Alexander to a fight. I even gave him his choice of weapons."

"So what happened?"

Willie said, "He chose his Pit Bull."

Mr. Bucks and the pet shop owner looked at the Samoyed.

"I want a dog which befits my social standing," said Mr. Bucks. "You say this one has an impeccable pedigree?"

"Quite," said the owner. "Why, if this animal could talk, he wouldn't speak to either of us."

Later that week, at a party on his estate, Mr. Bucks showed off the animal to his business rival, Mr. Cash.

"Yes," Mr. Bucks said, "this delightful little fellow has papers which trace his line all the way back to the days of Henry II. And yours?" he asked snootily.

"That's difficult to say," replied Mr. Cash. "All of my dog's records were lost in the Flood."

The president of the American Kennel Club was touring a breeder's estate when she encountered a little boy walking a dog.

"Do you know who I am?" she asked the lad.

"Yes, ma'am. You're the president of the American Kennel Club."

"Very good. And do you know how big the club is?"

The boy thought for a moment. "Yes, ma'am. Almost six feet tall."

The woman frowned. "Young man, we have thousands of members. How could they fit in a space like that?"

"I don't know," said the boy, "but my father is six feet tall and he's always putting his hand to his forehead and saying, 'I've had the American Kennel Club up to here!'"

"Is my Cerberus a good watchdog!" Caren said to her friend. "Why, just yesterday he prevented a fox from sneaking in and eating a meat pie I'd just baked."

"Chased the fox away, did he?"

"Nothing like that," said Caren. "He ate the pie himself."

Q: How is the letter y like a little dog's tail?

A: It's at the end of a puppy.

Q: What kind of dog did Sir Galahad own?

A: A mongrail.

Benchley enjoyed going to the hunting lodge each weekend. On one visit, he hired a dog named Riveter for $25 and was delighted with him. The dog sniffed out ducks, then energetically collected them once they'd been bagged.

The next week Benchley asked for Riveter. The master of hounds said, "Riveter is one of our most popular dogs, so we've decided to call him Super-Riveter—and must therefore charge you ten dollars more."

Benchley paid the money, had another superlative hunt, and the following week asked for Super-Riveter.

"Ah," said the master of hounds, "I'm afraid you wouldn't be happy with him."

"And why not?" asked Benchley. "He's been fine the last two weeks."

"I know," said the forlorn chap. "He was so good, in fact, that we decided to change his name to Foreman."

"And?"

"And now all he does is sit on his duff and bark!"

Then there was the dog who believed that the pest things in life are flea.

Curt and his dog Scruffy were hitching down the country road. When a man stopped, he said to Curt, "I'll be glad to give you a ride, but not your dog."

"That's okay," Curt said. "Scruffy's a real fast runner—he'll keep up with us."

The man was dubious, and when he started out he only did thirty-five. Unable to see out the passenger's side, he asked, "How's your dog doing?"

"Fine," said Curt. "He's right beside us."

Surprised, the man accelerated to fifty. "How about now?"

"Just fine," Curt assured him.

The man pushed the car to sixty-five. "Scruffy still there?"

"Not even breathing hard," Curt said.

Not sure he believed the boy, the man slammed on the brakes, got out of the car, and looked over the hood. He saw Scruffy standing there, his body flat as a pancake and his tail hanging from his mouth.

"What the hell happened?" the man asked.

Curt replied, "I said that Scruffy runs fast, but he never had to *stop* that quick before."

Q: What kind of dog gets up before all others?
A: Poodles. They wake curly in the morning.

Q: Why did Mrs. Bigger grow when a dog snapped at her?
A: Because she became a bit Bigger.

Churchill walked up to the other members of the fox hunt. Behind him walked a magnificent hound, stately with a glossy coat and alert eyes. Even the other dogs in the group were impressed.

"My word," said his friend Lord Wilkins, "that's a splendid-looking animal."

"That's Excelsior," Churchill said, "and I bred him myself. I trained him for a year to run, burrow, and chase down a fox faster than any hound that ever lived."

The other members of the group were keen to see the dog in action and, sure enough, when the hunt began, Excelsior was ahead of the pack in a shot. The fox, crossing a road, saw the lightning-fast dog approaching and froze. Excelsior bore down on him, but just as he grabbed the hapless animal a truck sped by and crushed them both.

Churchill ran over; both animals were dead. Lord Wilkins lay a comforting hand on his shoulder.

"Sorry, old chap. I know how disappointed you must be."

"That I am," said Churchill, "but not for me."

"I don't follow—"

"Excelsior was a proud dog," said Churchill. "Now, for all eternity, he'll think it was the bloody fox that killed him."

Q: Why are Eskimos the cruelest pet owners on earth?
A: Because they sleigh their dogs.

Q: Why did the timid puppy turn to stone?
A: Because it became a little bolder.

Bruce's mother gave him ten dollars to buy lunch for himself and his sister Terri at the diner down the street. On the way, they passed a man who was selling puppies for ten dollars each. Unable to resist, Bruce bought one, named it Elvis, and went home.

While he stayed outside playing with it, Terri went inside.

"Back so soon?" her mother asked.

"Yes," said Terri. "I'm afraid we never made it to the diner."

"Why not?"

"Because Bruce spent ten dollars on Elvis."

"Elvis?"

"That's right," said Terri. "He ate nothin', bought a hound dog."

DUCKS

Q; Why is a pet duck like a horse's tail?
A: Because they both grow down.

Q: Why did the duck put its head in the stream?
A: To liquidate its bill.

Q: Why did the duck leave the stream?
A: It had more interest in the bank.

Millie asked Billie, "Have you ever seen a man-eating duck?"
"No! Where can you see that?"
She replied, "At a Chinese restaurant."

Q: What kind of duck eats with its feet?
A: They all do: They're attached!

Q: What kind of duck is made of concrete?
A: None. We just threw in the concrete to make it hard.

Q: Why did Bart train his duck to fly upside down?

A: He wanted to see it quack up.

Brad and his father were visiting the children's zoo. Looking at the fowl, Brad asked, "Which do you think are faster, ducks or chickens?"

"Chickens," said his dad.

"How come?"

"Well, have you ever heard of Kentucky Fried Duck?"

Q: What do you call a duck that just doesn't fit in?

A: Mallardjusted.

The teacher was lecturing on history and said, "Can anyone tell me the genus and nationality of the first animal to circumnavigate the globe?"

Ellen raised her hand. "It was that duck from Paris, I believe."

The teacher's eyebrows arched. "*What* duck from Paris?"

Ellen said, "Sir—France's drake."

Jane sat beside young Dean, who was stroking his pet duck.

"What's its name?" Jane asked.

"Ben Hur," he replied.

"I guess you liked the book."

"Never read it," Dean said.

Jane's brow furrowed.

"See," said Dean, "I called the duck Ben, and then one day it started laying eggs. . . ."

Abigail was hiking through the country when she came upon a little boy and his duck sitting beside a pond. The pond was quite long and, rather than go around, Abigail said, "Do you have any idea how deep the water is?"

"Oh, it's real shallow," replied the boy.

Taking him at his word, Abigail started wading across. After taking three steps, she plunged into water that was well over her head.

After struggling from the pond, she stalked over to the boy. "I thought you said the water was *shallow*!"

"Heck, I thought it was," he said. "It only reaches to the bottom of my duck's belly!"

Rufus ran over to Buddy's house.

"My duck just laid an egg that was a *foot long*!"

"Pshaw," said Buddy, "my duck can beat that."

"Yeah? How?"

Buddy replied, "With an eggbeater."

Q: What kind of movie only stars waterfowl?
A: A duckumentary.

Q: What kind of ducks are found in Lisbon?
A: No ducks . . . just Portugeese.

Then there was the man who owned a cranky, elderly drake which he referred to as a darn old duck . . .

. . . and the artistic drake who sculpted a platypus, accurately described as duck-built . . .

. . . and the duck that refused to add four and four, 'cause it got ate . . .

. . . and the goose that was so frightened by a bolt of lightning it got people-bumps.

Q: What two states have the highest population of waterfowl?
A: North and South Duckota.

Q: What does a baby duck become when it goes in the water for the first time?
A: Wet.

Q: What waterfowl may one day claim the throne of England?
A: The duck of York.

Then there was the drake that never got to see a human face. Every time it flew over, someone yelled, "Duck!"

FROGS

Q: What's green and can leap ten feet in the air?
A: A frog with hiccups.

"Doctor!" shouted Leroy. "You've got to help my friend *fast*."
"Why?"
"He swallowed my frog."
"Well, that's certainly no catastrophe."
"Are you kidding?" said Leroy. "He may croak at any second!"

Then there was the boy who organized a frog baseball team because he heard they were great at catching flies.

Q: What's the difference between a baby frog and the month's rent?
A: One's a tadpole, the other a pad toll.

Q: What's the toughest time to try to catch a frog?
A: Leap year.

Dilbert had two frogs. He wanted to know their gender, so he took them to the aquarium.

"Young man," said the curator, "it's fortuitous that you brought them to me: I happen to be a frog expert, and there's a simple way to tell whether a frog is male or female. When you feed flies to it, you'll notice that the male frog only eats female flies, and the females only eat male flies."

"I see," said Dilbert. "And how do you tell which flies are male and which are female?"

The curator said, "How should I know? I'm a frog expert."

Rufus cared only about his pet frogs. He played with them in the afternoon, he slept with them in the evening, and he brought them to school each morning.

Dismayed by the boy's preoccupation, his teacher said, "Rufus—I'd like you to write a hundred-word composition for homework, and I *don't* want your frog to be in it."

The next day, Rufus came to school and the teacher asked him to read his assignment to the class. Standing in front of the room, Rufus cleared his throat and read, "My favorite pet ran away last night, so I stood at the pond and yelled, 'Here, froggy,

froggy, froggy, froggy, froggy, froggy, froggy,
froggy, froggy, froggy, froggy, froggy, froggy,
froggy, froggy, froggy, froggy, froggy, froggy,
froggy, froggy, froggy, froggy, froggy, froggy,
froggy, froggy, froggy, froggy, froggy, froggy,
froggy, froggy, froggy, froggy, froggy, froggy,
froggy, froggy, froggy, froggy, froggy, froggy,
froggy, froggy, froggy, froggy, froggy, froggy,
froggy, froggy, froggy, froggy, froggy, froggy,
froggy, froggy, froggy, froggy!' "

George was out for a stroll, his pet frog in his pocket, when he bumped into Mr. Wallace. Wallace was just leaving the bank and a wad of bills slipped from his pocket. George's eyes went wide when he saw the money, and he ran to pick it up.

"Say, Mr. Wallace," he said. "You know what the difference is between my frog and a fistful of money?"

"No, I don't," the man said impatiently.

George smiled and pressed the frog into Mr. Wallace's hand.

The frog was eating out by the pond when his owner suddenly appeared.

"Time to go home!" the lad said.

"Already?" croaked the frog. "Boy, time's sure fun when you're having flies."

Jason said to Sean, "I hear you have a frog that says its own name."

"That's right."

"I don't believe it! What's its name?"
Sean replied, "Ribbit."

Q: What are newborn frogs called in Switzerland?
A: Gstaadpoles.

Jeremiah said, "Mom, I'm going out to play!"
"Not with those holes in your pants!"
"No," he said. "With my frogs."

Q: What happened when the parrot mated with a frog?
A: She gave birth to a pollywog.

Orville said to Wilbur, "My sister is so dumb! She thought a tadpole is what's used to hold up small telephone wires."
Wilbur said, "What *does* it hold up?"

Q: What happened to the frog who planted himself in front of a fire hydrant?
A: He was toad away.

Then there was the frog who went to the doctor because he wasn't feeling jumpy.

Jenson was performing an experiment for a biology report.
"Jump," he said to the frog on the dissecting table. The frog did as it was told, and Jenson made a note in his journal. Anesthe-

tizing the animal, Jenson cut off one of its hind legs. When it awoke, he said, "Jump." The frog curled its remaining hind leg beneath it and made a valiant leap. Jenson noted that in his journal and, anesthetizing the frog again, removed its second hind leg. When the frog awoke, Jenson said, "Jump." The frog just lay there, and Jenson wrote in his journal, "The results are clear. When both legs are removed, the frog becomes deaf."

Quincy met Gail on the street.

"Bet you a quarter my frog can jump higher than a house," he said.

Gail took him up on the bet, and Quincy put the frog down. After some prodding, the animal jumped a few inches off the ground.

"Ha!" said Gail. "He *didn't* do it!"

"Ha, yourself," Quincy said as he picked up the quarters. "I won. The house didn't even leave the ground!"

Q: Why is the letter t like a frog?
A: You can find one in the middle of earth or water.

"What does a tadpole become when it grows up?" the teacher asked.

Benny answered, "Bigger."

Then there was the magic frog that perched on a lily pad and turned it into a toadstool.

Q: What's a frog's favorite game?
A: Croq-uet.

"Mama!" cried the baby frog from the shore, "help me jump to the lily pad!"
"No," said the mother frog, "You'll just have to hop to it."

Q: What kind of shoes do frogs wear in the summer?
A: Open toad.

Q: What did the frog collector say when he went to the doctor?
A: "Wart's up, doc?"

Q: What Chopin piece is like an army officer who's eaten a frog?
A: Etude in D major.

GOLDFISH AND OTHER WET PETS

Bertram walked into the pet shop.

"How much for a goldfish?" he asked.

"They're $2 apiece," said the clerk.

"And how much for a whole one?"

Q: Where do Superman's goldfish live?
A: In the Super Bowl.

Q: What fish do you find in the alphabet?
A: A minnow . . . in *l m n o p.*

"I'll bet you a quarter my goldfish knows how to subtract," Wally said to Esther.

The girl didn't believe him, and gladly agreed to the bet. When the coins were on the table, Wally tapped the fish tank.

"What's one minus one?" he asked.

The fish just swam around and didn't say a word.

"See?" said Esther. "The fish said *nothing!*"

Wally scooped up the coins. "Isn't that correct?"

Q: Where do Batman's goldfish live?
A: In the bat tub.

Q: Where did Albert Einstein keep *his* fish?
A: In a think tank.

Then there was Edgar Allan Poe, who was *sure* his pet bird was insane. Seems it was a raven.

Q: What kind of fish do you keep in a bird cage?
A: A perch.

The vacationing boys had caught a beautiful tropical fish on a golden Jamaican beach. To determine who got to keep it, they decided to see who had told the biggest lie in his life.

Mr. Charles, sitting nearby, overheard what the boys were doing and walked over.

"You know, kids," he said, "you should come up with a better way of seeing who wins the fish."

"What do you mean?" asked one of the children.

"Lying is dishonorable. Why, when I was your age, I never told a lie."

The kids gave Mr. Charles the fish.

Tommy said to Jennifer, "Know how you can communicate with a fish?"

"No. How?"

"You drop it a line."

Tommy then said, "Guess what? I just got a tuner fish."

"You mean a *tuna* fish."

"No," said Tommy, "a tuner fish. It's always playing its scales."

Not to be outdone, Jennifer asked, "Do you know which side of your fish has the most scales?"

Tommy said he did not.

"The outside," she replied.

Jennifer followed that up by asking, "Do you know why pet shop owners are so greedy?"

Once again, Tommy had no idea.

"Because their work makes them sell fish."

Q: Where do soldiers keep their pet fish?
A: In the tank corps.

Mrs. O'Brien didn't know quite how to tell her daughter that her goldfish Patty had died. She decided that the best approach would be a straightforward one, so when the girl came home from school Mrs. O'Brien stood in front of the girl, looked her straight in the eyes, and said, "Honey—I'm sorry to have to tell you, but Patty is dead."

The girl's eyes dropped and she nodded once, then walked grimly to her bedroom.

Mrs. O'Brien rose, pleased that the youngster had taken it so well. Suddenly an awful shriek came from the girl's room.

"Maaaa! Where's my *goldfish*?"

"Why—I just told you," Mrs. O'Brien said. "Patty's dead!"

The girl ran over and fell at mother's feet, a hysterical heap.

"I thought you said *Daddy*!"

Mindy told a friend, "When I'm down in the dumps, I get myself a new tropical fish."

The friend said, "I thought you got them at the fish store."

Q: What's the difference between a small, cute minnow and a tough little dog?
A: One's a pretty guppy, the other a gritty puppy.

Timothy loved fish so much that he decided he wanted to become a marine biologist when he grew up. Unfortunately, he wasn't able to get his grades above C level.

Then there was the fish fancier who claimed his pets' lives were ova before they began . . .

. . . and the man who collected goldfish and canaries, having always enjoyed fish and cheeps.

Q: When Herman got a second place to keep fish, what Egyptian ruler did he become?
A: Two-tank Herman.

Phoebe bought a goldfish, but when she got it home it just lay on the bottom of the bowl looking ashen. Taking it back to the pet shop, she said to the clerk, "Sir, I don't like the looks of this fish."

The clerk said, "Madam, if it's looks you want, you should've sprung for the tropical fish."

"My little brother got in trouble today," Burt said to Kirk.

"What'd he do?"

"He was feeding the fish."

"What's wrong with that?"

"He was feeding them to the cat."

Q: Why did the dummy put his goldfish under the mattress?
A: So they could swim in the spring.

"Betty, have you given your goldfish fresh water?"

"No, Ma," Betty said. "They didn't drink what I gave them last week."

Eddie wanted to raise fish, so he bought a few from the local fish store. Three days later, he was back.

"Fish doing all right?" the clerk asked.

"Not really," said Eddie. "They all died."

The clerk told him to make sure the water wasn't too hot or cold, and sent Eddie away with new fish.

Two days later, Eddie was back. Much to the clerk's dismay, the new batch of fish had died as well.

"I just don't get it," the clerk said.

"Me neither," said Eddie. "I watered 'em with warm water like you said. Maybe I'm just planting 'em too deep."

The teacher said to Len, "If I gave you two goldfish today, and three goldfish tomorrow, how many goldfish would you have?"

"Seven."

"Wouldn't you have five?"

"No, ma'am. I already have two."

The little boy was walking down the street when he saw a sign that said GOLDFISH SOLD HERE. He walked into the shop.

"I'd like to get goldfish 'cause I ain't got any," he said to the clerk.

The clerk looked down and smiled. "Young man, it's 'I *don't have* any . . . you *don't have* any . . . we *don't have* any.' Do you understand?"

"Yeah," said the boy, "but then why d'ya got that sign in the window?"

Q: What part of a goldfish is like the end of a book?
A: The fin is.

Mrs. Dundee came home to find her son dropping slices of bread in the bathtub.

"Why on earth are you doing that?" she asked.

"Because I want goldfish like the ones we have in school," the boy explained, "and the teacher said hers came from being bred in water."

Q: What kind of fish do Eskimo children have?
A: Coldfish.

Q: And French children?
A: Gaulfish.

Q: Why did the goldfish age?
A: It lost the *g*.

HORSES

Barbara asked the riding instructor, "What's the best way to mount a horse?"

"Dunno," said the wise guy. "Why don't you ask a taxidermist?"

Carter was out riding when he bumped into Mildred.

"I'll bet you twenty dollars that my horse can jump across the river," Carter said.

As soon as Mildred showed him the color of her money, Carter walked the horse across the river to the opposite bank, then had it jump.

Later, Carter bumped into Mildred back at the stable.

"How's your horse?" Carter asked.

Mildred glared at him and snarled, "Shut up."

Carter said, "You might try feeding him prunes instead of apples."

What do you call . . .

. . . a horse that shares its stall with worms? *An Appleloosa.*

. . . a claim to determine a colt's father? *A palomino suit.*

. . . a horse that'll only eat cheese? *A Mousetang.*

. . . a pair of thieving horses? *Bonnie and Clydesdale.*

. . . a horse that's bad to the bone? *George Thoroughbred.*

. . . a horse that's had cosmetic surgery? *A Lipozaner.*

As they stood watching their thoroughbreds run, millionaire Tate told his daughter, "See that horse over there? He's been running races for two years now."

"Wow!" said the girl. "He must be *exhausted.*"

"For years," said Wyatt, "I was a cowboy, roping all the wild horses in Chicago."

"Chicago?" said his companion. "But there *are* no wild horses in Chicago."

"Sure," said Wyatt. "Not any*more.*"

Jim was walking down the country lane when he saw a man standing inside a horse van, pulling frantically on the reins of a huge stallion. The animal was half inside and seemed disinclined to go farther.

"Could you use a hand?" Jim asked.

"Thanks, yes," said the man, and Jim ran over. He grabbed the other side of the reins and began tugging.

After ten minutes, the horse hadn't budged.

"I quit," the man said to Jim. "I'll never get this horse into the van."

"Into the van?" Jim said. "I thought you were trying to get him *out!*"

Mr. Marlow was strolling through the country when he saw a stable with the most beautiful steed he had ever laid eyes on. It was seventeen hands high and white, with rippling muscles and a fine, flowing mane.

Driving to the house, Marlow struck a deal to buy it from the owner—who did, however, pass on one key piece of information.

"We are a religious family, Mr. Marlow, and we've instilled those values in our horse. To get him to gallop, you must say, 'Thank God.' To get him to stop, you must say, 'Our Father, who art in heaven.' "

Settling into the saddle, Marlow whispered, "Thank God," and the animal took off. They rode for miles when suddenly a cliff loomed ahead. Unfortunately, Marlow couldn't remember the phrase to make the animal stop and tried every biblical passage he could think of until, just feet from the edge of the cliff, he shouted, "Our Father, who art in heaven!"

The animal ground to a stop.

Shaking and perspiring, Marlow reached into his pocket and pulled out a handkerchief. "Thank God," he said as he mopped his brow.

Chutney came walking up to the patio, where his friend Chauncey was sitting and sipping tea.

"Good day," said Chutney. "What have you been doing on this delightful morning?"

"I've been riding."

"Ah, horseback?"

"Of course," said Chauncey. "In fact, he got back an hour before I did."

Grimsby and a friend were leaning against the barn door.

"Y'know," Grimbsy said wistfully, "I wish I had the money to buy a hundred horses."

His friend said, "Now, what would you do with a hundred horses?"

"Not a thing," said Grimsby. "I just wish I had the money."

Q: What disease did the cowboy get after trying to break his new horse?
A: Bronc-itis.

Q: How do you hire a horse?
A: Put it on a stepladder.

Then there was the breeder who decided that it cost less to feed horses than any other animals, since they ate the most when there wasn't a bit in their mouths . . .

. . . and the senator who retired to a ranch, thus going from filibuster to filly buster.

Q: How do you make a slow horse fast?
A: Take away its oats.

The woman asked the riding instructor, "Is this horse well behaved?"

"Indeed he is. Why, whenever he comes to a fence, he always lets the rider go over first."

Steadman ran up to the stable owner.

"Your horse kicked me in three different places!" he yelled.

"Claptrap," said the owner. "He's been in the same stall all day."

Q: Who did the breeder summon when his thoroughbred was possessed by the devil?
A: An exhorsist.

Duke entered a curio shop in Texas, and his eye was drawn to the skull of a horse.

"What's that?" he asked the proprietor.

"That," said the woman, "is the actual skull of Betsy, the horse which Davy Crockett rode to the Alamo."

"How much is it?"

"Ten thousand dollars."

"Hmmm . . . that's a bit too expensive for me," said Duke.

The woman reached under the counter and

pushed a smaller skull into his hands. "This one is only two thousand dollars," she said.

"Whose is it?"

"It's Betsy's," she said, "but when she was a filly."

Then there was the woman who opened a horse hotel to provide the animals with a stable environment . . .

. . . and the breeder who kept racing horses. Naturally, the horses always won.

Glen had a horse named Sarah, which he loved very much. Alas, Glen eventually had to sell her due to a musical hangup: When she was exposed to the moonlight, Sarah neighed.

HORSE QUIZ

Use horse sense to answer these challenging questions:

Q: Can a horse tied to a ten-foot tether walk twenty feet from a tree?
A: Yes, if the tether isn't tied to the tree.

Q: What's as big as a horse, but weighs nothing?
A: Its shadow.

Q: If a horse was born in Connecticut, lives in New York, takes ill in Pennsylvania, and dies in Ohio, where is it buried?
A: In the ground.

Q: What kind of horse has six legs?
A: One that's being ridden.

Q: How many horses have three legs?
A: All of them.

Q: Why is it difficult to recognize horses from behind?
A: Because they often switch their tails.

Upon graduating from college, the young attorney decided to specialize in cases involving horses. As it happens, he was in great demand after winning a case in which a hard-of-hearing stallion was hit by a bus. Needless to say, he capitalized on his success by advertising himself as the world's foremost deaf horse lawyer.

Q: Why did the horse run away from the stable?
A: It heard it was to be shod at dawn.

Q: How did the timid horse avoid participating in a joust?
A: He got the knight off.

Q: What do you use to buy a horse?
A: Horse cents.

Griswold inherited a billion dollars, but he wasn't very bright. Sensing this, Mackie the gambler cornered him at the VIP lounge of the track.

"Isn't that your horse Stylish racing down there?" Mackie asked.

"Yes, it is."

"Bet you a grand he loses."

Griswold agreed to the bet and the men looked up at the TV monitor. Sure enough, Stylish lost. After Griswold paid up, Mackie gave him a chance to win his money back: He bet Griswold another grand that Stylish would lose again.

And so he did.

Feeling bad for him, Mackie said, "Listen— I gotta tell you, dodo, that second race was actually an instant replay . . . a tape of the first race."

"I know," said Griswold, "but I didn't think Stylish would lose *again*!"

Q: What's the most important part of a horse?
A: The mane part.

Mitch said to his five-year-old, "Well, son— how did you like going to the zoo?"

"I loved it, Dad," the boy said. "Especially when one of the animals paid ten to one."

Q: What's the hardest part about learning to ride a horse?
A: The ground.

It was Sally's first day at the stable.

"Excuse me," said the riding instructor, "but you're sitting backward in the saddle."

Sally said down her nose, "How do you know which way I'm going?"

Mrs. Fletcher walked up to the butcher. "Do you sell horse's meat here?"

"If they come in with their owners, why not?"

"My horse had a terrible fall," one rancher said to another.

"Gee, that's too bad."

"Yeah," said the rancher, "but I'm hoping the winter'll be better."

Q: What's the difference between a tailor and a groom?
A: One mends tears, the other tends mares.

"I didn't know what to do," the rider said to his instructor. "The horse wanted to go one way, and I wanted to go another."

"What did you do?"

The rider said, "He tossed me for it."

Then there was the bronco buster who acquired a wild horse for a million bucks . . .

. . . and the good-natured horse whose motto was, "Any friend of yours is a palomino."

Little Nellie watched the stable hand shoe the horse.

"Hey, mister," she said. "When you're finished with that horse, could you build one for me too?"

Q: Why did the mama horse feel sick?
A: It had a very bad colt.

Q: Why should you put on a horse's right shoes first?
A: Because it's better than putting on the wrong ones.

"I see you're putting up a new stable," one rancher said to the other.

"Yes. I find it counterproductive to put up an old one."

The insurance agent was interviewing a prospective client.

"So, you're a cowboy. Have you ever met with any accidents?"

"No—never."

"That's strange. It says here that you were hospitalized three times last year. For what?"

"I break broncos for a hobby. Sometimes I smash a rib or two when they throw me."

The agent frowned. "Then how can you possibly say you've never have any accidents?"

"I *haven't*! Those danged horses threw me on purpose!"

Q: What do you call a lawman who's always getting bucked off his horse?
A: The thrown ranger.

The cowboy walked into the tack shop.

"How much for a pair of spurs?" he asked the sales clerk.

"Forty dollars."

The cowboy looked in his wallet, thought for a moment, then pulled out a twenty.

"I'll take one spur."

"What'll you do with just one?" the clerk asked.

The cowboy replied, "I figger if I can get one side of the horse movin', the other side'll go too."

Randi inherited a ranch, but she didn't have the vaguest idea about how to mate horses. Phoning the National Horse Information Bureau, she asked, "How long should the male and female horses be kept together?"

"Just a moment," the representative replied.

"Thanks," said Randi, and hung up.

Gunnar entered the empty diner at two in the morning, sat at the counter, and waited.

When no one came to take his order, he began shouting.

"Hey! What's a guy have to do around here to get some grub? Die of starvation?"

Moments later, a horse came through the swinging doors. "Jesus," said the animal, "can't I even do the dishes without some whacko raising a ruckus? Where you in a rush to get to at this hour, anyway?"

Gunnar said nothing, just stared at the talking horse.

"You got a problem, mister?" the stallion asked, wiping his hooves on an apron.

Gunnar continued to stare.

The horse came over and looked down at the customer.

"Mister, I said—you got a problem?"

"Yeah," Gunnar said. "What happened to the nice cow that used to run this place?"

Q: What do you give a nauseous horse?
A: Plenty of room.

"Daddy," said the little girl, "I've got my eye on that lovely horse at the stable."

"Good," said her father, "because you'll never get your bottom on it."

Then there was the man who exclaimed, "There's nothing like riding for three hours to make you feel better off."

"Mom," said Harold as they crossed the city street, "I want to go horseback riding."

"But Harold," she said, "where will you find a horse in the middle of Cleveland? And how can we afford it?"

"Just buy Tampax," he replied.

"What?" his mother cried.

"Tampax. It says on TV that you can use it to go horseback riding whenever you want."

Mr. Amana knowingly asked his daughter Ginger what she'd like more than anything in the world.

"A baby brother or sister," the girl replied.

Sure enough, over the next few weeks, Ginger noticed her mother growing rounder and rounder—until, after nine months, her brother James was born.

While visiting her mother and brother in the hospital, Ginger took her father aside.

"Now, Dad," she said, "there's one more thing."

"What's that, honey?"

"If it wouldn't be too uncomfortable for mom, do you think I can have a horse next?"

Then there's the horse breeder who describes himself as a man who can raise horses without lifting them . . .

. . . and the man who refused to describe his beast of burden as a cart horse, since he'd always been told never to put the cart before the horse.

The math teacher asked Barney, "How many legs would you find on ten horses?"

Barney replied, "Twenty-four—"

"I'm afraid that's not right."

"I wasn't finished," Barney said. "Twenty fore and twenty rear."

Q: Why is a bronco like an egg?
A: Because you can't use it unless it's broken.

Q: What's the difference between a racehorse and a commuter?
A: One trains for runs, the other runs for trains.

One little boy said to another, "Y'know, Mr. Mulligan is a magician!"

"What do you mean?"

"Well, when he rode from the stable, I heard him say he was going to turn his horse into a trail!"

Actually, Mr. Mulligan wasn't all that amazing . . . or smart. As he was out riding, he came to a very low tunnel cut into a mountainside. His horse was too big to fit through it, and since he couldn't go around, he picked up a rock and began smashing away at the top of the tunnel to make it larger.

After several minutes, a state trooper happened by. He asked Mr. Mulligan what he was doing, and after Mr. Mulligan explained, the officer grew angry.

"Why the heck are you wrecking the tunnel? All you need to do is dig up some dirt along the bottom!"

Mr. Mulligan shot back, "That shows what *you* know! It's not his legs that're too long—his head's too high!"

Not-very-bright Clancy and Nancy bought horses, but since their animals' features were quite similar and they were stabled side by side, the couple were worried they wouldn't be able to tell them apart.

"I know," said Nancy. "Let's braid the mane of one of them."

"Good idea," said Clancy.

As luck would have it, the two misunderstood who was to have the horse's mane braided, and both had it done.

"Now what?" said Clancy.

After thinking for a moment, Nancy said, "I know! Why don't you just remember that yours is the white one, and mine is the black one?"

Q: What's the difference between a man whipping up hot fudge topping, and one who builds a home for his stallion?
A: One makes a sauce for his table, the other makes a stable for his horse.

Bill was riding through the countryside when his horse suddenly stopped. No matter what he did, it refused to budge, and eventually he was forced to dismount. Walking to a nearby cottage, Bill was greeted by a bent old woman.

He explained the problem and asked if he could use the phone to call the stable.

"No phone here," said the crone, "but don't despair." She plucked a vial from a shelf and handed it to Bill. "Give him a sip of this potion, and your horse will surely move."

"How much is the potion?" Bill asked.

"Five dollars," said the woman.

Bill paid her, returned to the horse, and fed it the potion. In a flash, the animal's eyes went wide and, whinnying loudly, it took off down the road.

A minute later, Bill was knocking at the cottage door.

"Did the potion work?" the hag asked.

"It did indeed," said Bill. "Now will you please give me ten dollars worth so I can *catch* him?"

"Out West," the cowboy told the dude, "I used to chase cattle on horseback."

"Incredible," said the dude. "I didn't know that cattle rode horses."

Victor said to a friend, "My dad's a sorter at a thoroughbred breeding farm."

"Wow," said the friend, "that sounds important. What does it mean?"

"It means," said Victor, "that he sorter cleans out the stables."

Doris visited Duke in the hospital.

"I heard you were hurt by your horse!" she said. "Were you thrown?"

"No," said Duke, shrugging painfully. "I'm here because it behooved me."

Q: What's the difference between a lost horse and a broken-down horse?
A: One can't find its way back, the other is one.

Q: How is manna from heaven like horse hay?
A: Both are food from aloft.

Q: Why was the Queen of England's horse the least expensive animal in history?
A: Because it was bought for a sovereign.

Each weekend Mr. Brown went out hunting, and his oblivious wife stayed home watching TV. One day Mrs. Brown said that *she* wanted to go out hunting. Although she knew nothing about guns and even less about animals, she pestered her husband until he agreed. He gave her a rifle, showed her how to use it, then offered her some advice.

"Sad to say, there are a lot of hunters out there who will see a lady and try to get her game. If you *do* bag a deer, stand by it with your gun and don't let anybody near."

The couple entered the forest and went their separate ways. After a while, Mrs. Brown saw a deer near a tree. She aimed, fired, and it went down. The woman hurried over, but no sooner had she arrived than a big, angry-looking man burst from the trees on the other side of the carcass.

The woman raised the gun. "This is *my* deer," she said menacingly.

The man stopped and raised his hands. "Okay, lady, if you say so. But would it be all right if I took my saddle?"

MICE

Q: What's the difference between a chimp cage at the zoo and a rodent that lifts weights?
A: One's a monkey house, the other a hunky mouse.

The teacher said, "Bobby, spell *mouse*."
"M-o-u-s."
"Yes . . . but what's at the end of it?"
"T-a-i-l."

Q: Why did the young boy buy a mouse?
A: He wanted a pet that would squeak when spoken to.

Q: What do you call false teeth for mice?
A: Rodentures.

Sitting himself down at the bar, Densmore lay his hat on the counter, ordered a beer, drank all but the last few sips, then poured the rest in his hat. He did the same with his second, third, and fourth beers.

Watching from a nearby stool, Morrison said, "Mister! Howcome you keep spillin' the last drops of beer into your hat?"

Densmore glowered at him. "Mind your own business, pal, or I'll knock your block off."

Suddenly a woozy mouse leapt up from the hat and snapped, "Yeah, an' that goes for your cat too!"

Q: How did the mouse feel after the cat chased it through a screen door?
A: Strained.

The teacher said, "Ira, can you name something that's four feet by four feet by four feet?"

"Sure," said the lad. "A mouse behind a chair waiting for the cat to go away."

One mouse said to the other, "I think I finally got this scientist trained."

"Oh?"

"Yeah. Every time I go through the maze, she gives me cheese."

The English teacher said, "The poet Robert Burns loved mice. Indeed, this love compelled him to write, 'To A Field Mouse.' "

"Cool," Babs said, snickering. "Did he ever get a reply?"

Mrs. Finch called the exterminator.

"There's a mouse somewhere in the kitchen, and I'm so afraid of it I can't even go in there. Why, in one week I've lost ten pounds! I want you to come over next week and dispose of them."

"Next week?"

"That's right," Mrs. Finch replied. "I've got another ten pounds to lose first."

Actually, Mrs. Finch was lucky: Not all exterminators make mouse calls.

When her husband came home, Grizelda blubbered, "I—I found a mouse in the oven today."

"No kidding! What did you do?"

"I went and got your gun."

"And—"

"When I came back, it was out of my range."

Q: How did the rodent save his companion from drowning?

A: Mouse-to-mouse resuscitation.

NASA designed a new kind of harness for the seats in the space shuttle and, building a miniature version, they strapped a mouse in the seat. They whipped him around in a centrifuge, shot him across the desert in a rocket sled, and ejected him from an airplane.

When the mouse was returned to his cage, another mouse walked over.

"So, how was it?"

"Rough," said the astromouse, "but I'll tell you one thing."

"What?"

"It beats the hell out of cancer."

Q: What does a Russian call his pet mouse?
A: Comrat.

Q: What's the difference between a mouse scurrying up a staircase and one just looking up?
A: One steps up the stairs, the other stares up the steps.

"Gee," said the mouse to his mate, "I just had a terrible experience. There I was, munching on a map, when this guy came along, angry as can be."

"What'd he do?"

"What do you think?" said the mouse. "He tore the routes out."

Doug's father said, "Why did you put a mouse under your sister's pillow?"

"Because she would have seen a bear trap," Doug replied.

Q: What's the difference between someone playing solitaire and a hungry mouse?
A: One finds it an ease to cheat, the other finds cheese to eat.

Warren phoned the front desk of the hotel. "There's a mouse on my pillow!" he cried.

"Don't worry," said the concierge. "The cat under the covers will get it."

The teacher said, "Olaf, finish this rhyme: Hickory, dickory, dock, the mice ran up the clock. The clock struck one—"

Olaf replied, "But the rest of them managed to get away."

Q: What's gray and has four legs and a trunk?
A: A mouse going on vacation.

Q: What happened to the mouse that fell off the shelf and landed in a glass of Pepsi?
A: Nothing. It was a soft drink.

Q: What do hard bread and a mouse ducking into its hole have in common?
A: With bread, you see it's stale. With the mouse, you see its tail.

Then there was the mouse that plunged into an ordinary stew and transformed it into ratatouille . . .

. . . and the cowboy who had a pet mouse and rodent to town . . .

. . . and the mouse who ate too much cheese and became gnawseous.

Q: What's the difference between volcanic stone and a bunch of rodents waking in the morning?
A: One's pumice, the other up mice.

PARROTS AND PARAKEETS

Q: What geometric shape is like a missing parrot?
A: A polygon.

Bored, the parrot opened its cage at the pet shop, took a $50 bill from the cash register, and waddled over to a nearby restaurant.

When the waiter came over, the bird said, "I'd like chopped sirloin, please—marinated in lime water, topped with onions sautéed in a nice basil sauce, and sprinkled with sesame seeds."

"Of course," said the waiter.

The bird arched a brow. "Excuse me, but—don't you find any of this *unusual?*"

"Not at all," replied the waiter. "That's how I like chopped sirloin myself."

After returning to the shop, the parrot ambled over to the owner. Interrupting a conversation the man was having with a customer, the bird asked, "Where'd you put *The New Yorker*?"

"It's in the lavatory."

When the bird had hip-hopped off, the patron said, "I'm impressed!"

The shop owner snickered. "Don't be. He only reads the cartoons."

Miller's wife had always wanted a parrot, and for their fortieth anniversary he searched for a special one. He finally found what he was looking for.

On the long-awaited day, he presented the bird to his wife. She was thrilled, and began tapping the bars of its cage go get it to talk.

"Uh, darling," Miller said, "I must tell you, there's good news and bad news about this bird."

"What's the good news?" she asked, still tapping the bars.

"Well—this parrot lays eggs which are fully half the size of its body."

"That's incredible!" she gasped. "What's the bad news?"

Miller took his wife out of earshot so as not to hurt the parrot's feelings. But before he could answer, they noticed the bird begin to shiver. Its little face contorted, its wings flew wide, its head turned up, and it began to shake so hard that the sounds of the rattling cage filled the house. Then, slowly, the bird began laying a huge egg.

As the couple watched with amazement,

Miller said, "The bad news is that the parrot only says one word."

"What's that?"

Just then, the egg rolled to the floor of the cage. Panting and utterly wasted, the bird opened its beak and the couple heard it mutter, "Oww . . . oww . . . *oww!*"

Q: What do you call a very old parrot?
A: Grandfeather.

Q: What do you call a crime boss's parrot?
A: Godfeather.

Mallory walked into the pet shop. "I'd like to buy a talking parrot."

"Certainly sir," said the shopkeeper, who showed him to a cage he kept in the back. Inside was a distinguished-looking bird with a steady gaze and smooth green feathers.

"Speak, Bartlett," said the shopkeeper.

"Money is the root of all evil," the bird said in a cultured British voice. "Beauty is in the eye of the beholder. There is nothing to fear but fear itself."

The shopkeeper said proudly, "Pretty impressive, no?"

"Yes," agreed the customer. "How much?"

"One thousand dollars," said the shopkeeper.

"Hell," said Mallory. "For that kind of money, I want a bird that writes his own stuff."

There was a knock on the door, and the parrot said, "Who is it?"

"Exterminator," said the voice from outside.

"Who is it?"

"Exterminator."

"Who is it?"

"I said it's the *exterminator*! You called about termites—"

"Who is it?"

"It's the exterminator, dammit! Did you or did you not call?"

"Who is it?"

Furious, the exterminator kicked the door in, but the exertion was too much and the poor man keeled over dead.

Moments later, the master of the house arrived. "Good gracious! Who is it?"

The bird said, "The exterminator."

Q: What do you get when you mate your pet parrot with a gorilla?

A: A bird that says, "Polly want a cracker— and *fast*!"

Mrs. Black bought a parrot, and all that the young male bird did was curse, curse, and curse. She happened to mention her problem to Father Revere at the church, who said he *might* have a solution.

"I have a pet parrot too," he said, "but she is the model of propriety. All *she* does every day is sit on her perch and pray—hour after hour, nothing but silent, gentle prayer. If you bring your parrot over, perhaps she will have a rehabilitating effect on him."

Mrs. Black was willing to try anything, so she brought the bird over and Father Revere put the rough-speaking bird in his own pet's cage. The rowdy parrot swaggered over to the praying bird, whose eyes were shut, her wings folded in supplication.

"Hi, honey!" he said. "Wanna have a good time?"

The lady parrot opened her eyes. When she saw the brawny male, her beak turned up in a smile.

"At last!" she cried, "just what I've been *praying* for all these years!"

Little Louie wanted a parrot in the worst way. Unfortunately, the pet shop was sold out of parrots.

"I wanted a bird that *talks*," wailed Louie.

"Best I can do is a woodpecker," said the owner.

"But woodpeckers don't talk!"

"True," said the owner, "but then, how many parrots know Morse code?"

The snooty English teacher brought her parrot back to the pet shop.

"It uses improper language," she complained.

"But madam," said the owner, "that's impossible! No one in this shop *ever* used foul words."

"Who said anything about foul words?" the teacher huffed. "She misplaced a modifier."

Then there was the lonely parrot who left its cage for a lark.

Q: What kind of words are used by most parrots?
A: Pollysyllabic.

Q: How would you describe a parrot that sounds like a donkey?
A: A bird brayin'.

Q: What do you call a circus consisting entirely of parrots?
A: A Beak Top.

Gribowski was upset because his parrot wouldn't speak, so he brought him back to the pet shop. The owner told him that the bird couldn't talk because its upper beak was a tad too big.

"Just file the tip off, and the bird will talk its head off."

Gribowski went home, but a day later he was back to buy another bird.

"What happened?" the clerk asked. "Didn't you do as I said?"

"Never even got that far," said Gribowski. "Goddam vise killed him!"

What's the name of . . .
. . . the movie based on the life of Buford Pusser's parrot? *Squawking Tall.*
. . . who played the parrot? *Bird Lancaster.*
. . . the novel about the blind macaw? *Parrot Eyes Lost.*
. . . the all-parrot rock group from England? *Polly McCartney and Wings.*

No doubt about it: Henry was henpecked. When he finally divorced his wife, he lost everything but his prized crested parrot . . . and even that was subject to joint custody. Henry had him in the morning and early afternoon, his wife at night.

Or to paraphrase the judge, it was "Cockatoo till two!"

Hegel the parrot was clever, but teenager Dwight was smarter. He took the parrot with him when he went to college, then called his father.

"Dad," he said, "the English prof thinks Hegel is a genius. For an extra grand, he says he'll teach him fluent English."

The money was sent, and a week later Dwight called again.

"Dad, the literature prof thinks he can teach Hegel to read. Want to risk another grand on it?"

The additional money was sent. Finally, it was time for Dwight to come home for vacation. When he arrived without the bird, his father was alarmed.

"Where's Hegel?" he asked.

The boy took his father aside. "Dad, it was awful. One night Hegel looked up from his history book and said, 'Hey—is your dad still bringing his secretary home for lunch?' I got so mad, I strangled the little bugger."

"You—you *killed* Hegel?" his father gasped. "Sweet Hegel?"

"Had to."

"But I loved that bird."

"Sorry, Dad."

His father said, "And you're *sure* he's dead?"

Mrs. Fawcett was visiting her old friend Mrs. Gancher when little Everett walked in with his pet parrot.

"What a beautiful bird!" Mrs. Fawcett said. "Where's it from?"

"Africa," said Everett.

"What part?"

Everett replied, "All of him."

Q: What's the difference between a hand-held two-way radio and a parrot that waddles around its cage muttering to itself?

A: Nothing. They're both walkie-talkies.

Mr. Flanders had worked hard to put his son Field through college. Upon graduating, the young man got a job with the State Department. He rose quickly through the ranks and was soon appointed ambassador to Brazil.

Upon arriving, he looked for a suitable gift to send to his beloved father. The elder Flanders enjoyed Broadway music, and when Field found a parrot that could sing the entire repertoire of Al Jolson he didn't flinch at the thirty-thousand-dollar price tag. After paying for it, he had it sent to his father.

A week later, Mr. Flanders phoned his son. "I can't thank you enough for the bird," he said.

"You really liked it, Pop?"

"Oh, yes," his father said, "it was *delicious*."

"I want to return this parrot," the man said to the pet shop owner. "Every day for a week, I stood in front of his cage and said, 'Can you talk, little parrot?' For six days he just glared at me without saying a word."

The owner said, "Sir, you knew the terms of sale. We guarantee our parrots will talk, but we don't guarantee when."

"It isn't that," the man said. "This bird's got a chip on his shoulder."

"A chip?"

"That's right. On the seventh day I walked up to the cage and said, 'Can you talk, little parrot?' And he looked me square in the eye and said, 'I can talk, you pain in the ass. Can *you* fly?' "

Q: What do you call a fidgety parakeet?
A: A fuss-budgie.

Q: What do you get if you mate a parrot and a shark?
A: An animal that talks your ear off.

Then there was the wealthy parrot fancier in the Netherlands who had his pets' homes made from money. You might say that each parrot was a bird in a guilder cage.

Q: What do you call a bird that enlists in the military?
A: A parrot trooper.

"You want to see a marvelous bird?" said the pet shop owner.

"Indeed I do," replied Mr. Whipple.

The owner took him to a parrot which had a piece of string tied to each leg.

"Watch," said the shopkeeper as he tugged the first string. The bird whistled, "Give My Regards to Broadway." When the owner pulled the second string, the parrot whistled "Forty-five Minutes to Broadway."

"That *is* amazing," said the man. "What happens if you pull both strings simultaneously?"

The bird replied, "I fall off my perch, jerk."

Q: What do you get when you cross a parrot and a swine?

A: A bird that hogs the conversation.

Q: What do you get when you cross a parrot with a parrot?

A: A bird that's been double-crossed.

Q: What do parrots say on the Fourth of July?

A: "Polly want a firecracker!"

Eddie showed up for work an hour early. When his boss arrived, she smiled.

"I see you took my advice and got a new alarm clock, Eddie."

"Actually, Ms. Clark, I kept the old one."

"But I thought you couldn't hear it?" she said.

"I couldn't . . . and still can't. But I bought a parrot that hears the alarm, and what he says when it goes off would be enough to wake the dead!"

Q: What do you get when you cross a pigeon with a parrot?

A: A bird that apologizes for the mess it makes.

The devout Gibbons family had many pets, for they loved all of God's creatures . . . including their parrot, who had an unfortunate habit of uttering profanity. The only time that proved to be a problem was when the local priest stopped by the house during his Sunday walk. On those occasions, the Gibbonses simply put the bird in the closet, where there was no one to talk to.

One beautiful spring Wednesday, the priest decided to take a walk. He stopped by the Gibbonses, and as he came up the walk, Mrs. Gibbons told the children to put the bird away. They did so quickly while Mrs. Gibbons admitted the priest.

As the woman and the clergyman walked past the closet, a muffled voice said from inside, "Short friggin' week, wasn't it?"

Q: What kind of birds love to recite poetry?
A: Parrokeats.

Q: While we're on the subject of special birds, which one loves to solve crimes?
A: Hercule Parrot.

Then there was the singing bird who wrote an operetta entitled *The Parrots of Penzance* . . .

. . . and the inventor who created special shoes for birds that kept falling off their perches. He called his invention paracleats.

RABBITS

Q: Why did the young boy eagerly await his first math class?
A: He wanted to see if he'd enjoy multiplying as much as his rabbits did.

Rodney walked up to his mother, weeping his little eyes out. Cradled in his arms was a tiny white ball of fur.

"Ma," he said, "my rabbit is dead."

The woman looked down at the animal. "I'm so sorry," she said. "Why don't we bury it out back? Then we'll go to the mall and get you a nice big milk shake."

Suddenly the fur twitched in Rodney's hand.

"Wait," his mother said, lifting one of the rabbit's ears. She saw an eyelid flutter and said, "Rodney, look! The rabbit's not dead!"

Looking down at the precious bundle in his arms, the boy cried, "Let's *kill* it!"

Q: What's the name of the celebrated novel about waterfowl that raise bunnies?
A: *Rabbitry Ducks.*

Q: What do you call the unexpected death of a pet rabbit?
A: Premature hare loss.

Q: What's the name of the comedy team that's a hit at barnyards across the nation?
A: Rabbit and Cowstello.

Q: What's the difference between an insane rabbit and a counterfeit bill?
A: One's a mad bunny, the other bad money.

Lao Wu, a student in a Beijing high school, was asked to report on the rabbits he was raising.

"They just gave birth," he said, "and the newborn bunnies are all devoted Communists."

"That is good," the teacher replied.

Five days later, Lao Wu was asked to report again on the rabbits.

"The newborn bunnies are doing well," he said, "and they are now capitalists."

The teacher frowned. "Five days ago, you said they were Communists, Lao Wu."

"Yes, madam," said the boy. "However, now their eyes are open."

Then there was the magician who had to postpone his show: He'd just washed his hare and couldn't do a thing with it.

Q: What time is it when there are a pair of foxes trying to get at your dozen pet rabbits?

A: Two after twelve.

Three boys entered Milton's Pet Shop.

"I'd like five dollars worth of rabbit food," said the first boy.

Since Milton didn't get much call for rabbit food, he kept the pellets in a container way up on the top shelf. After dragging over the ladder, climbing, scooping out the food, carefully weighing it, and returning the extra pellets, he put the ladder back in the storeroom and turned to the second boy.

"What would you like?" Milton asked.

"Five dollars worth of rabbit food," said the second boy.

With a sigh, Milton went back to the storeroom, got the ladder, climbed to the container, and once again measured out five dollars worth of rabbit pellets. He stood by the foot of the ladder and glanced at the third boy.

"I suppose you want five dollars worth of rabbit food as well?"

"No," said the boy.

"Good," said Milton, and he dragged the ladder back to the storeroom. When he returned, he asked the boy, "What can I get you?"

The lad replied, "Two dollars worth of rabbit food."

Q: Why did the Wall Street investor buy up all the young hares he could find?
A: The time was right for a leveret buyout.

You might say, in fact, that the investor was just lapin 'em up.

Q: Who was the most powerful rabbit in Roman history?
A: Julius Caeshare.

Q: When did that rabbit die?
A: On the Ides of March Hare.

Mindy asked Barb, "Do carrots really improve your eyesight?"

"I guess so," said Barb. "I've never seen a rabbit with glasses."

Q: What's the difference between a bunny and a lumberjack?
A: One chews and hops, the other hews and chops.

Q: What's the difference between an athletic rabbit and a slightly demented one?
A: One's a fit bunny, the other a bit funny.

Q: What's the difference between a sensitive spot in your elbow and Peter Cottontail's AT&T unit?
A: One's a funny bone, the other a bunny phone.

Mrs. O'Hare met Mrs. Rabbitowitz in the carrot patch.

"I hear you had bunnies," Mrs. O'Hare said.

"Yes, and they're lovely. Very sweet and full of frolic."

"Ah." Mrs. O'Hare smiled. "It's so nice to hear that you're one big hoppy family!"

Q: What do you call rabbits that marched in a long, sweltering Easter parade?
A: Hot, cross bunnies.

Q: How do you make a rabbit stew?
A: Keep one waiting.

Then there was the rabbit who found two dozen meals growing in a circle . . . a beautiful twenty-four-carrot ring!

Q: What do you get when you cross a frog and a hare?
A: A bunny ribbit.

Q: What can you put in front of a rabbit to get your hands on it?
A: The letter *g*.

The farmer said to the shipper, "It's imperative that this milk get to the city while it's still fresh. How do I know your trucks are *really* fast?"

"Well, sir," said the shipper, "all I can say

is that the last farmer we worked for shipped two rabbits with us—and it was two rabbits we delivered."

Then there was the breeder who came up with a means of getting his hares to market even faster. He called it rabbit transit.

Q: Where do you send a rabbit with a broken leg?
A: To the hopspital.

Q: What's invisible and smells like carrots?
A: A bunny burp.

Q: How do bunnies stay in shape?
A: Hareobics.

SKUNKS

Q: What kind of awards are given to owners of pet skunks?
A: Pewlitzer prizes.

Q: What do many of those Central Europeans *call* their skunks?
A: Polecats.

Speaking of Poles, the Polish gentleman noticed that his pet skunk wasn't as frisky as usual, so he put her in the car and drove her into town.

"Doc," said the Pole, "there's something wrong with Pepper."

The man behind the counter glanced at the animal, then at its owner. "Looks fine to me." He studied the skunk's master. "But you know . . . there's something wrong with *your* eyes."

"Really? How can you tell?"

"The sign outside says JEWELRY."

Q: What's the difference between an activist and a skunk breeder?
A: One raises a stink, the other lots of 'em.

Q: What's the difference between a skunk owner with ESP and the skunk?
A: One's got a sixth sense, the other a sick scent.

Q: Where do Central Europeans bathe their pet skunks?
A: The Oder.

"Hear you had a bit of weather here t'other day," Barney said to Andy.

"We had a full-fledged hurricane."

"How strong was it?" asked Barney.

"Barn, it was so strong my skunk let out the same smell four times in a row!"

Q: Why did Raymond encourage his pet skunk to go into show business?
A: Because she was always the scenter of attraction.

Elliot was a music student who wondered if William Congreve's old adage was true: Did music have charms to soothe a savage breast?

With his keyboard in hand, he went to the woods and began playing. In less than a minute, he'd attracted a crowd of animals, all of them sitting quietly and listening to him play.

Suddenly a big skunk ambled over and released a potent blast of odor all over the keyboard. Elliot left in a flash.

Holding their noses, the other animals looked at the skunk.

"What'd you do *that* for?" asked a deer. "I was enjoying the concert."

The skunk replied, "I don't know about you, but I can't *stand* it when someone can't do a decent arpeggio!"

Winslow asked, "Mommy, why do skunks smell?"

His mother answered, "So they can tell if the milk is fresh."

Sherry took her skunk to the fast food restaurant. Unfortunately, they weren't able to order a thing. Sherry forgot her money, and the skunk was no help: It only had a scent.

Mr. Lawrence went to see the marriage counselor.

"I can't stand it anymore!" Lawrence screamed. "My wife insists on keeping her pet skunk in the room, and it's more than I can bear! It isn't fair, I tell you. Why should I have to sleep in a stuffy room with that smelly creature?"

"Why don't you compromise?" asked the counselor. "Try opening the window."

"What?" balked Lawrence. "And let my bats escape?"

Roderick stormed over to his neighbor's house.

"What do you mean, telling everyone in the neighborhood that I'm a complete idiot and that I smell like your pet skunk!"

The neighbor said, "I *never* said that you smelled like my skunk."

Terence said to a coworker, "Y'know—I've heard that only really smart people keep skunks for pets."

"That's right. Why, I have a pet skunk myself."

"Hmmmm," said Terence. "So much for that theory."

Q: What are the most commonly used letters in the skunk alphabet?
A: P.U.

Then there was the skunk owner who put his pet on a boomerang and ended up with a smell that won't go away . . .

. . . and the missionary who found himself surrounded by skunks. He got down on his knees and said. "Come, let us pray—" and immediately wished he hadn't.

Q: What has four legs and flies?
A: A dead skunk.

"Mom," said Wendy, "Gerry gave me a skunk!"

"I'm sorry, but you can't keep it in the house. What about the smell?"

Wendy said, "Oh, the skunk won't mind."

Q: Truth be told, how many skunks does it take to smell up a house?
A: A phew!

Ridley said to his friend, "I went out into the woods yesterday and caught two skunks. By the time I got home, I also had two fish."

"You mean you stopped by the pond?"

"No," said Ridley. "I still had the two skunks . . . and two smelt."

Calvin said to Winnie, "Have you heard about the baby that was raised on skunk milk?"

"Yucch, no! What kind of baby would drink that?"

"A baby skunk," said Calvin.

Q: What's the best way to describe a skunk's odor?
A: Distinctive.

Q: What's the difference between cash borrowed from your mother and the price of a skunk?
A: One is money owed her, the other odor money.

The animal fancier spinster Gruber said to a friend, "My dog snores, the parrot swears, the cat stays out all night, and most of all my pet skunk is free to roam the house. What on *earth* do I need a husband for?"

Q: What do dyslexics do when they see a skunk?
A: They go up.

SNAKES

Milton called the vet.

"Doc, you've gotta help me! My snake just ate the TV remote control!"

"I'll be right over."

"Great, but what do I do in the meantime?"

The vet answered, "Read a book."

It was pet day at school, and Matt brought in his pet snake.

"Why did you decide to have a snake for a pet?" the teacher asked.

"Simple," Matt answered. "We were out in the woods one day, and it scared my sister."

The biology teacher asked, "Can anyone tell me three members of the snake family?"

Roger raised his hand and said, "The mother, the father, and the baby."

"I hear you found a baby snake stranded in your garage," Rhonda said to Ralph. "What kind of shape is it in?"

Ralph said, "Long and tubular."

Then there were the two boa constrictors who had a crush on each other.

What do you call a snake that . . .
. . . cleans vindows? *A viper.*
. . . eats everything with mustard? *Ana-condiment.*
. . . wants to squeeze Mrs. Derek or Mr. Jackson? *A Bo constrictor.*
. . . falls in love with another snake? *An asp kisser.*
. . . tells the president of the United States what to do? *A Bushmaster.*
. . . can give you sums? *An adder.*

Q: What's the difference between an NBC news anchor and a hooded snake?
A: One's a Brokaw, the other a cobra.

Q: Why did the man call his pet snake Lava?
A: Because he was always moltin'.

The teacher said, "Raymond, can you use the words *bitter end* in a sentence?"
"Sure," said Raymond. "My mom bent over near my snake, and it bitter end."

Pamela asked the class nerd, "Where do you think snakes go when it gets cold out?"
"Search me."
"Thanks," she said, "but I'm not *that* curious."

Giving an oral report on his pets, Wendell said, "I've got six snakes at home: Do, Re, Fa, So, La, and Ti."

"What happened to 'mi'?" asked the teacher.

"Gee—you're mean, Mrs. Stalb, but you're no snake."

Q: What do you call a deadly snake with a lovely singing voice?
A: A choral snake.

The sword swallower Georges DeGrasse mistook his pet Boa for a sword and swallowed it. He began to choke, but by the time the doctor arrived it was too late. The sword-swallower had expired.

As the physician said upon pronouncing him dead, "There's very little one can do about a snake in DeGrasse!"

Q: What do you call a snake who graduates at the head of its class?
A: Phi Beta Copperhead.

In biology class, the teacher asked, "What kind of snake eats the least?"

Abraham answered, "A dead one, ma'am."

Then there was the snake who gave birth to a bouncing baby Boa . . .

. . . and another who traveled from coast to coast in order to make a long-distance coil.

Q: On what holiday is it correct to eat snake?
A: Fangsgiving.

Q: What's the worst way to handle a rattlesnake?
A: Being there in poison.

Mitzy asked her friend, "Would you rather a snake attacked you, or a rat?"
The friend replied, "I'd rather the snake attack the rat."

Q: How do snakes end a spat?
A: They hiss and make up.

Q: Why is it a bad idea to have 288 snakes?
A: They're just too gross.

Roger came running up to Liz in the woods. "A snake just bit me in the leg!"
"Which one?"
"I don't know!" he cried. "They all look alike to me!"

Q: What is a snake's favorite Beatles song?
A: "Venom Sixty Four."

The Cockney man walked into a bar, put his rattlesnake on the counter, and proceeded to drink while the viper gnawed at his sleeve.

The bartender watched for a moment, then asked, "Say—doesn't that hurt?"

The man smiled and said, "Naw . . . there's no 'arm in it."

The survival instructor said, "What steps should you take if you're being chased by a rattlesnake?"

A pupil answered, "Very long ones."

The teacher said, "Reginald—name an animal that crawls on the ground."

"A snake."

"Very good. Wilbur, now you name one."

Wilbur replied, "Another snake."

One snake said to the other, "I forget. Are we poisonous?"

"Why?"

"Because I just bit my tongue."

Q: How can you tell if a snake is a baby?
A: It plays with its rattle.

Q: What do you call a snake that becomes a Canadian law officer?
A: Mountie Python.

The teacher said, "Class—how many feet would you have if you had a five-foot snake and a three-foot snake?"

"None," said Rufus. "Snakes don't have feet."

Q: What do you call a well-behaved snake?
A: A civil serpent.

Q: Why is the letter *a* the unhappiest letter of all?
A: It's always in the midst of snakes.

TURTLES

Elroy was tired of his pet turtle, so he sat outside the house behind a small table with a sign on it: TURTLE FOR SALE, $1.00.

As his father was leaving for work, he said to the boy, "Elroy, take it from your dad—you've got to think big. Try to get more money for the turtle. If you can't, *then* lower the price."

Elroy added three zeroes to the price, then sat and waited.

When his father came home, Elroy was just packing up the table; the turtle dish was nowhere in sight.

"Son," he said, "where's the turtle?"

"Gone," he said.

The man was amazed. "Did you really get a thousand dollars for it?"

"Sort of," Elroy said. He reached into his pockets and said, "I swapped 'im for these two five-hundred-dollar frogs!"

Then there was the bratty kid who said to his dad, "Buy me a turtle, and make it snappy!"

"I hear you found a turtle on Main Street," Oscar said to Oliver.

"That's right."

"What was he doing there?"

Oliver replied, "About half a mile an hour."

Arthur walked into the restaurant. "Will you bring a little turtle soup?"

"I'm sorry, sir, but we can't seat turtles, regardless of their size."

"What's the name of your turtle?" Melody asked Wanda.

"Ginger."

"Does she bite?"

"A little. She's a cookie."

"A cookie?"

"Yes," said Melody. "Ginger snaps."

Mason walked into the pet shop with a turtle in his hand. The clerk looked up and said, "What are you doing in here with that disgusting thing?"

Mason said, "I'll have you know, you fool, that my turtle is cleaner than you are!"

The clerk snorted and replied, "That's who I was talking to."

One turtle passed another in the field.

"Where ya goin'?" asked one.

"To McGillicut's barn. He's got a nice garden."

"Yeah," said the other, "but this is winter, pal. There're no flowers now."

The turtle resumed inching along. "There will be by the time I get there."

Clark walked into the pet store, where he saw a sign that read MAGIC TURTLES.

"What kind of magic does the turtle do?" he asked the clerk.

"Simple. You buy one, put it in your coat pocket, and—viola! You'll be smarter."

The turtle cost $25, but Clark desperately wanted to be smarter, so he paid the price. He put it in his coat and walked around town. After three hours he didn't feel any different and returned to the pet shop.

"You tricked me!" he screamed at the clerk. "This turtle doesn't make you smarter!"

"Sure it does," said the clerk. "You're smarter now, aren't you?"

Q: If Arnold Schwarzenegger made a movie with Michelangelo, Donatello, Leonardo, and Raphael, what would it be called?
A: *Turtle Recall*.

Then there was the boy who dressed his turtle in a people-neck sweater.

Q: Why did the turtle cross the road?
A: To get to the Shell station.

The boy's mother looked at her sons as they nursed bloodied fingers.

"Well, have you learned *never* to go near snapping turtles at the pond?" she asked.

One of the boys said, "Yes, Ma. It really tortoise a lesson."

A MENAGERIE

BARNYARD ANIMALS

Q: What kind of pets are pigs when they first wake up from a nap?
A: Ham stirs.

Then there was the man who took his pet sheep for a walk and got a ticket for making a ewe-turn . . .

. . . and the dyed-in-the-wool sheep breeder: He was killed when the herd stampeded . . .

. . . and the man who kept sheep as pets for the shear pleasure they brought . . .

. . . and the sheep breeder whose wife left him because he was always talking chop.

Q: What did the mother turkey say to her disobedient children?
A: "If your father could see you now, he'd turn over in his gravy!"

Estelle's pet turkey died of old age and, as a tribute to the bird, she decided to eat it for Thanksgiving. Since she'd never prepared a turkey, she called the local butcher and asked what to do with it.

"Did you buy it here?" the butcher asked.

"I've only bought fish from you, sir," Estelle said, "never a turkey."

She explained that the bird had been her pet for years, and after listening to the story the butcher said, "Madam, you should stuff your bird."

Estelle gasped, then said, "And you may be certain, sir, that I shall never buy anything from you again!"

Q: Why does the boy call his pet pig "Ballpoint" whenever he's in the sty?
A: That's his pen name.

Then there was the man who had a pet owl that went "Cluck cluck" and didn't give a hoot . . .

. . . and the man who bought a goat to serve with toast, 'cause he heard it was the best butter there is.

Q: Why did Ernest Hemingway's chicken cross the road?
A: To get to the author's side.

When his goat had babies, farmer Paar refused to sell any of the young goats to rival farmer Carson.

"But I'm offering you a fortune for those scrawny little animals!" said Carson. "You've got to be joking!"

"No," said Paar, "I kid you not."

Q: What do a coward and a hen's egg have in common?
A: They both chicken out.

"I hear you got a pet henway," Jesse said to Chris.

"Huh? What's a henway?"

Jesse said, "About a pound."

Q: Why did the man buy a pet rooster?
A: He wanted an alarm cluck.

The sheep rancher said to the dude, "Do you realize it takes four sheep to make one sweater?"

"Migosh!" the dude replied. "I didn't even know they could knit."

Q: Why did the mason feed concrete to his chicken?
A: He was hoping to turn the bird into a brick layer.

Then there was the dim architect who thought a flying buttress was a female goat with wings . . .

. . . and the woman who kept track of her farm's steer population with cattle logs.

And do you know why that woman was keeping track of her cattle? NASA wanted them for a shuttle flight, which would have made them the first herd shot 'round the world.

The rancher from Lubbock decided to breed sheep as well as cattle. However, he had a novel idea: By feeding the animals various food dyes, he'd be able to color the wool *before* it was sheared. The plan clicked, making the rancher the biggest lamb dyer in Texas.

Q: Who does a sheep call when it wants to be sheared?
A: A baa-baa.

Q: What happened when the farmer crossed a pig with an owl?
A: The owl gave her dirty looks.

Then there was the shepherd whose sheep were stolen by a crook . . .

. . . and the sheep thief who went by the name of Ali Baa Baa . . .

. . . and the Mexican farmer who cried "Olé!" when his chickens went on strike.

As it happens, the reason the fowl struck is because they were tired of working for chicken feed.

The city slicker asked the farmer, "Do you really think I can milk your cow?"
"Sure," said the farmer. "All it takes is a jerk."

Q: Why did the chicken walk all the way to town?
A: It wanted to see Gregory Peck on stage.

Q: What do you call a cow that's just had a baby?
A: Decalfinated.

The city girl was visiting the farm, and got up at dawn. She walked into the barn, where the farmer was sitting on a stool and milking the cow.
"I've always wondered how that was done," the girl said, then asked how long cows should be milked.
The farmer answered, "The same as short ones, dear."

Q: Why did the Eskimo buy a cow?
A: She was out of cold cream. (Did that make the cow an Eskimoo?)

Q: What do you get when you cross a chicken and a hyena?
A: An animal that laughs at every yolk.

Abel was visiting his brother Seth.
"I see that your neighbor Randy doesn't let his chickens run loose in your yard anymore."
"Nope. I took care of that."
"How?" Abel asked.
"Simple. I painted an egg gold, slipped it in my garden, and made sure Randy saw me find it."

Q: What do you get when you cross a hen with a cow?
A: Roost beef.

Q: What do you call chickens from another planet?
A: Eggstraterrestrials.

Melanie was driving through the country when she stopped short. Her eyes opened wide as she saw a four-legged chicken dart in front of her car.
Pulling up to the farm on the side of the

road, she walked up to a farmhand who was sweating and breathing hard.

"Sir," Melanie said, "I just saw the most amazing thing! A chicken with four legs!"

"I know," said the hand. "Since most people like to eat drumsticks, we genetically engineer them that way."

"Incredible! But tell me—do they taste the same a regular drumsticks?"

The farmhand wiped his brow with his sleeve. "Don't know, ma'am. we haven't been able to catch one yet."

Q: Why did the cow jump over the moon?
A: The milkmaid's hands were cold.

Then there was the militant hen who went to Kentucky Fried Chicken and kicked the bucket.

Q: How do chicks get out of their shells?
A: They egg-sit.

The farmer was bragging to another farmer, "I've got three hundred sheep."

"That's a lot of sheep," said the other farmer.

"And I've got four hundred chickens."

"That's a lot of chickens."

"And thirty bulls."

The other farmer said, "That's a lot of bull."

The commuter's car broke down and, late for his train, he began running. When he reached Farmer Joe's field, he said, "Would you mind terribly if I cut through your field? I've got to catch the 7:10."

"I don't mind," said Joe, "but if my bull spots you, you'll catch the 6:40."

Q: What does a compulsive shopper have in common with an angry bull?
A: They charge everything.

A man walked up to Farmer Patterson.

"What's the value of that big prize sheep of yours?"

"That depends," said Patterson. "Are you the tax man or did you run her over?"

Asked to write a composition entitled "What I'm Thankful For on Thanksgiving," little Timothy took pen in hand and wrote, "I am thankful that I'm not a turkey."

Q: What goes peck, peck, boom?
A: A chicken in a minefield.

Q: What kind of cow plays the violin?
A: Jascha Heifer.

"Milk is going up again," said the farmer.

"Shut up," said his wife, "and get the cow off her back!"

Q: Why does Sweden have so much cattle?
A: Because they believe in keeping Stockholm.

Then there was the farmer who crossed a cow with a mule to produce milk with a kick in it . . .

. . . and the other farmer who put a sign in the chicken coop: EMPLOYEES MUST WASH HENS.

Q: What did the chicken prove by crossing the busy road?
A: That it had guts.

A: Who killed the most ducks in the works of Shakespeare?
A: Hamlet's uncle, for he did "murder most foul."

Then there was the farmer who called his hen Macduff, because he wished her to lay on.

The chickens were pecking around by the fence when all of a sudden a softball came sailing into the yard.

"Gee," said one of the hens, "will you just *look* at the work they're turning out next door?"

The next night, a citrus fruit flew over the fence and rolled into the coop. Waking the next morning and seeing it beside him, a chick declared, "Wow! Look at the orange Mama laid!"

Q: What article of clothing does a well-dressed hog wear?
A: A pig's tie.

Q: Why do white sheep eat more than black sheep?
A: Because there are more of them.

Then there was the novice farmer who couldn't understand why anyone would bother to kill a pig and *then* cure it . . .

. . . and the farmer who didn't bother putting a bell on his cow, since he figured she already had two horns . . .

. . . and the hen who called her son Daylight, since he never sets.

Rich had never been to the city, and he'd never seen a movie. Unfortunately, when he got to the box office he left without buying a ticket: The sign said NO PETS ALLOWED, and he couldn't figure out how to get in without his calves.

Q: Why don't roosters need luggage when they travel?
A: They only take their comb.

Q: How does a cow multiply?
A: By mooing, because then it's a cow heard.

Q: How do cattle travel?
A: Steerage.

Farmer Monty encountered a shepherd in the field.

"Wow," said Monty, "those are lovely-looking sheep. Romanov?"

The tyro replied, "Yes, sir. All over the field."

When Farmer Francis Burton retired, former customers were surprised to see this sign posted to the fence: FARM STILL OPEN FOR BUSINESS! FRANCIS BURTON JR. SELLS PIGS LIKE HIS FATHER.

Q: Why did the lawyer drag the sheep into court?
A: He wanted to suet.

Q: What's the worst thing about flying a kite on a cow pasture?
A: Having to run into the wind.

Why did . . .

. . . the turkey cross the road? *It was the chicken's day off.*

. . . the cow cross the road? *To visit its fodder.*

. . . the hen cross the road halfway? *To lay it on the line*.

. . . the pig cross the road? *It wanted to be a road hog*.

Q: What do you get when you cross a kitten with a chicken?
A: A catapoult.

Then there was the dumb farmer who had two chickens. When one of them became ill, he killed the other to make chicken soup for it.

Q: Why did the farmer plant the letter *g* all over his field?
A: Because it turned oats into goats.

Q: What's the difference between a mugger stabbing a person and a farmer stabbing a pig?
A: One is assaulting with intent to kill, the other is killing with intent to salt.

The health inspector walked up to Farmer Abbott.

"Look," said the inspector, "you've got pigs walking in and out of your kitchen, chickens wandering through the bathroom, and sheep in the bedroom. This isn't *healthy*."

"Like hell," the farmer protested. "I ain't lost an animal yet!"

Q: What's the difference between a pig and a hillbilly?
A: The Ohio River.

Q: Finally . . . why did the chicken *really* cross the road?
A: Because it was a for-layin' highway!

BUGS

Q: What do you call a drone that leaves the apiary?
A: A bee leaver.

"How did you get a swollen nose?" Arnold asked.
"I bent down to smell a rosbe," said Blanche.
"A *rosbe*? There's no *b* in rose," Arnold replied.
"There was in this one."

Q: What's the difference between an actor and a mosquito?
A: One wants to get on the screen, the other around it.

Q: What do you call bugs that live in an ant farm?
A: Tenants.

Then there was the beekeeper who bred his bees with cattle and ended up with hivestock.

Q: What did the bee say to the flower?
A: "Hi, bud!"

Q: And what did the flower answer?
A: "Buzz off!"

"You're late," the teacher barked at Peter.
"Sorry, sir. I had to say good-bye to my pets."
"How long can it take to do *that*?" the teacher demanded.
"Well, sir, I've got an ant farm. . . ."

Q: What did the queen bee say to the disruptive drones in the field?
A: "Beehive yourselves!"

Q: What's a bee's favorite piece of music?
A: A pollenaise . . . unless it's in bee-flat.

Q: Which insect is always the healthiest one in the apiary?
A: The vitamin bee one.

"I hate this stuffy hive," said one bee to another.
"I know what you mean," said the other bee. "It's swarm in here."

Q: Why did the hiker wear shoes with rippled soles?
A: To give the ants a fifty-fifty chance.

Then there were the overworked termites that decided to take a coffee table break . . .

. . . and the termite who walked into a tavern and yelled, "Hey! Is the bar tender here?"

Q: Why did the ant race along the boxtop?
A: It said TEAR ALONG DOTTED LINE.

Jerry and David were watching the ants in the ant farm.

"Can you imagine what it would be like if those ants were the size of a house?" said David.

"Say . . . I know how to make a bug big," said Jerry.

"How?"

"All it has to do is eat me."

"Eat *you*?" said Jerry.

"Sure. Just me. Then *i* would be in it, and *u* wouldn't."

Q: What does a beekeeper have in common with a tenacious teenager?
A: One watches bee-laboring, the other practices it.

Q: What's the difference between those bees and the teenager?
A: The bee gets the honey, the teenager the whacks.

Q: What's the difference between a pop singer and a hurt beekeeper?
A: One is Sting, the other stung.

"If you were a caveman," Carlton asked Andy, "what kind of pet would you have had?"

Andy replied without hesitation, "A saber-toothed tiger. They were mean."

"Bet they couldn't have beaten the pet *I* would have had," Carlton said. "A bug."

Andy scoffed. "What bug could have beaten a saber-toothed tiger?"

Carlton replied confidently, "A ma moth."

Q: What do bees do with the honey they make?
A: Cell it.

Q: Which is easier to spell: *bees* or *ants*?
A: *Bees*. It's spelled with more *e*'s.

Using tweezers, beekeeper Ray plucked the spectacular bee Beauty from his apiary and went to hand it to a colleague, Arty.

"Are you sure you want to part with this treasure?" Arty asked.

"Yes," said Ray. "Beauty is a great organizer. Once your drones have been regimented, you can bring Beauty back."

However, Beauty had other ideas. As soon as the bee was clear of the apiary, it wriggled from the tweezers, flew up, planted its stinger in Ray's eyelid, and refused to budge.

As Ray gently tried to coax the bee out, Arty ran to the phone to call the hospital. "Send an ambulance, quick!" he cried.

"What's the emergency?" asked the dispatcher.

Arty replied, "Beauty is in the eye of the bee holder."

Q: What do you call an ant that breaks out of the ant farm?
A: Truant.

Q: What do you call an old, old ant?
A: An antique.

Q: Why did the firefly cross the road?
A: Because the light was with her.

FOREST ANIMALS

The billionaire had a petting zoo built in the backyard for his young son. As they approached the deer, the man said, "Son—do you know what animal that is?"

The boy said he did not.

"Let me give you a hint," said the man. "What does Mommy call Daddy?"

The boy looked at the animal. "So *that's* a cheating sonofabitch!"

Q: What do you call a blind deer?
A: No eye deer.

Q: What do you call a blind deer with four broken legs?
A: Still no eye deer.

The forest ranger said to the trainees, "What would you do if you were being chased by an adult grizzly?"

One trainee said, "I'd climb a tree, sir."

"But bears can climb trees," the ranger replied.

"Not this one," said the trainee. "It'd be shaking so bad the bear wouldn't get off the ground."

As it happens, the forest ranger didn't trust bears one bit. Every time he approached a bear's den, he felt sure there was something bruin.

Q: What did the beaver say to the log?
A: "It's been nice gnawing you."

Charlton had a fox in his yard and wanted to capture it as a pet for his daughter. But the creature proved elusive, so he consulted his neighbor Ben, who was a great outdoorsman.

"I'll tell you how to get 'im," Ben said. "Each morning, go to the mouth of the fox den and leave a strip of bacon and a piece of pie. Do this for a full week. At the start of the second week, just leave the bacon and wait."

"What'll that do?"

"When the fox comes out and demands to know what happened to the pie, you grab 'im."

Q: Why did the porcupine keep an alarm clock?
A: She was a stickler for punctuality.

After eating the last leaf of the tree, the mama bear said to the papa bear, "How does it feel to have played Captain Kirk?"

"Captain Kirk?"

"Yes. That's the final frond, dear."

Ripley said to his son, "Did I ever tell you the story about my forebears?"

"Nope," said the boy. "Just about the three bears."

As the family car was driving through the park, one bear said to another, "How awful to keep them caged up like that!"

Then there were the bears who wanted to start a newspaper just for grizzlies. Unfortunately, they couldn't find any cub reporters.

They did find a hunter, though, and one of the bears chased him back to town. It was the first time in the history of the village that someone had run down Main Street with a bear behind!

Then there was the boy who didn't understand why male deers didn't have unclers instead of antlers . . .

. . . and the newlywed who got rid of his pet bear because he feared it would eat his honey . . .

. . . and the man who took a picture of a giant grizzly tumbling off a cliff. The next day, the newspaper headlines announced, BEAR FALLS! WITNESS!

The teacher asked, "Is it true that trappers used to get fur from bears?"

"Yes," Leroy responded, "and the further, the better."

The teacher didn't have any better luck when she said, "Class, who can tell me where you can see deer born?"

Leroy answered, "Michigan, I think."

Then there were the buck and the doe who got together to have a little fawn . . .

. . . and the master of forest etiquette who wrote a column called Deer Abby (advising bucks and fawns alike what kind of behavior was deer rigueur).

Q: What is the pet of choice in New York City's western borough?
A: The Staten Island ferret.

Q: Why is a woman rich if she purchases ten female and ten male deer?
A: Because she's got twenty does and bucks.

JUNGLE ANIMALS

Q: What kind of pet *loves* snack food?
A: A chip monk.

Edsel wanted to work in the circus, and told the owner he would do *any* job just for the thrill of being part of the big top action.

The owner invited him to the show that night, and Edsel stood at his side as a beautiful young woman walked into a lion cage, cracked a whip, then stood statue-still as a fierce lion padded over, licked her face, and walked away.

The owner turned to Edsel. "Think you could do that, boy?"

"Heck," said Edsel, "no problem at all. But first you've got to take the lion out."

"Ah," said one lion to another as the safari bus rolled into view. "Meals on Wheels!"

Q: Why do giraffes have so much trouble apologizing?
A: It takes them a long time to swallow their pride.

"I'm so upset," Alex said to a friend. "My chimp took off its cage door and ran away."

"How did it do that?"

"He used a monkey wrench," said Alex.

Then there was the pet shop which sold chimpanzees and offered a monkey-back guarantee . . .

. . . and the tycoon who had a sudden urge to buy a pet from Africa. He called a friend who ran a preserve, only to discover that the lion was busy.

The Roman patrician spent a fortune keeping lions as pets and setting them loose on prisoners in the arenas. While watching the awful spectacle one afternoon, he turned to a companion and said with great satisfaction, "You know, Marcus, there's nothing I like better than seeing the lions eat up all the prophets."

Q: What's the difference between a prince and a mama monkey?
A: One's an heir apparent, the other a hairy parent.

ODDS AND ENDS

Q: What are the most musical pets you can own?
A: Trumpets.

Q: What kind of pets do nothing but lie around the room?
A: Carpets.

Q: Where did the Russian czars buy animals for their children?
A: In Petrograd.

Jennifer ran crying to her mother.
"Mommy, my hamster is gone!"
"Gone? How did that happen?"
"I was cleaning the cage and it vanished!"
"What were you cleaning it *with*?" her mother asked.
Jennifer replied, "The vacuum."

The carpet layer was finishing up in the living room when he noticed a lump in the middle of the carpet. Thinking he must have dropped his Snickers bar, and not really wanting to tear the carpet up again, he simply went over and hammered it down.

Just then, little Richie wandered in. "Mister," he said, "did you happen to see my hamster?"

Q: What do you call a newborn *cavia procellus*?
A: A beginuea pig.

Q: What did the boy name his singing salamander?
A: Wayne Newt.

Q: What was the salamander's equally melodious brother called?
A: Eft Sharp.

Q: Why did the boy give away his big pet anteater?
A: It was just too much aardvark to care for.

Then there was the boy who bought an aardvark for a pet because he heard they never got sick: It had something to do with being full of anty-bodies.

Even odder was the boy who swapped his lunch sausage for a sea bird. When he got home, his mother couldn't believe he'd taken a tern for the wurst.

Stranger still was the pundit who explained that the Arabs have so much oil because they use camels instead of cars.

Garth found two pigeons freezing in a snowbank, so he took them home and nursed them back to health. One of the pigeons became fit and was up and about in a few days; the other not only refused to fly, it just sat around the house preening.

Finally Garth had had enough of the vain, slothful bird. He went to it and said, "If you don't start flying, I'm going to take a piece of string, tie you to the other bird, and let him drag you through the yard!"

That did the trick. The bird was up in a flash, chirping, "I'll do whatever you say, only don't let me become pigeon-towed!"

Q: What kind of bird was a popular pet in Camelot?
A: The Knightingale. (Their singing sure made for a lot of sleepless knights! And *why* did they sing so much? To drown out all the lyres at court. Arthur any additional sections to this joke? No . . . no Uther parts.)

Q: What three keys have legs and can't open doors?
A: Monkeys, donkeys, and turkeys.

Q: What did Zeus say when he came down from Olympus looking for his favorite swan?

A: "Take me to your Leda."

"I can get a brand-new pet by standing outside during a thunderstorm," Max said to Rita.

"What kind of pet will you get?"

"Rain, dear," he answered.

Q: What did Noah say as he watched the animals climb onto the ark?

A: "Now I herd everything!" (Incidentally, did you know that Noah kept the bees in Ark hives? And that the worms didn't come in pairs, but in apples? And that the elephant took up the most space because it brought a trunk?)

Q: How did the pastor feel when his belfry was cleared of varmints?

A: Not bat.

Q: What do nomads use to hide their dromedaries in the desert?

A: Camelflage.

Q: What desert animal is always changing colors?

A: A camel-eon.

Q: Where do camels go when they want cream for their coffee?
A: The dromedairy.

Why did the . . .
. . . aquatic mammal cross the road? *To get to the otter side.*
. . . the hawk cross the road? *To prove it wasn't chicken.*

Then there was the man who bought a pet bison and got stuck with a hefty buffalo bill . . .

. . . and the scientist who crossed a crocodile with an abalone. He had *hoped* to create a small, powerful abadile. Alas, what he ended up with was a big crocabalone!

The woman walked up to the travel agent. "I'd like a ticket to Montreal," she said.
The agent checked through his files. "The only way we can get you there is via Buffalo. Will that be all right?"
"Sure," said the woman, "as long as the saddle's comfortable."

Young Stanley sat down to place an order with an exotic animals mail-order company.
"Please send me two mongooses," he wrote. He looked at it for a moment, crossed it out, and wrote, "Please send me two mongeese." He looked at that, then crossed it out and

wrote, "Please send me a mongoose. And while you're at it, send me another one."

Q: Why did the pelican refuse to alight in the water?
A: On account of the sea weed.

A Scotsman was touring Minnesota and stopped at an inn. While he was registering, he noticed a moose wandering about the grounds.

"Tell me," the visitor said to the proprietor, "what animal would that be outside?"

"That," said the owner, "is a moose."

"Hoot-man," said the Scotsman. "An' are your cats the size of elephants?"

Then there was the exhausted kangaroo that was out of bounds . . .

. . . and the mother kangaroo who was stressed out because it was raining and the kids would have to play indoors.

Indianapolis Colts tackle Marv Buckley always wanted to be a rancher, and after retiring he set up a place in Montana. Naturally, he was thrilled when some of his former teammates came to visit.

The men looked around and were surprised to find not a single head of cattle.

"Nice spread," said one, "but where're the animals?"

"They're dead," said Buckley. "Don't know why, but each one died when we were putting on our Double Horseshoe Rootin' Tootin' Lazy Spur Colts Aplenty Ranch brand."

Mr. Hastings called his vet.

"Joe," he said, "this ferret of mine has really gotten ferocious. Chews on his cage bars, menaces the other ferrets, eats all their fish. I just don't know what to do."

"Well," said the vet, "I know you won't put him to sleep—so why don't you take him to the zoo?"

Mr. Hastings did just that, and when he returned he phoned the vet.

"Did you do what I suggested?" the vet asked.

"Oh, yes," said Mr. Hastings. "And we had so much fun that tomorrow I'm taking him to the circus!"

PET KNOCK-KNOCKS

Knock-knock.
Who's there?
Wooden.
Wooden who?
Wooden you like to buy a kitten?

Knock-knock.
Who's there?
Arthur.
Arthur who?
Arthur any more frogs in the pond?

Knock-knock.
Who's there?
Burton.
Burton who?
Burton a cage won't sing!

Knock-knock.
Who's there?
Manuel.
Manuel who?
Manuel be sorry if we don't clean up the dog's
    mess!

Knock-knock.
Who's there?
Aloysius.
Aloysius who?
Aloysius that my parents would get me a dog.

Knock-knock.
Who's there?
Arnold.
Arnold who?
Arnold dog is no fun to play with.

Knock-knock.
Who's there?
Yukon.
Yukon who?
Yukon lead a horse to water, but you can't
    make it drink.

Knock-knock.
Who's there?
Lena.
Lena who?
Lena little closer to my snake, why don't you?

Knock-knock.
Who's there?
Scold.
Scold who?
Scold out, so I let the dog in.

Knock-knock.
Who's there?
Tennis.
Tennis who?
Tennis too many goldfish for that small tank.

Knock-knock.
Who's there?
Armageddon.
Armageddon who?
Armageddon a new guinea pig 'cause the old
    one died.

Knock-knock.
Who's there?
Phyllis.
Phyllis who?
Phyllis tank, I got a new goldfish.

Knock-knock.
Who's there?
Athena.
Athena who?
Athena tropical fish I've just *got* to buy!

Knock-knock.
Who's there?
Dewey.
Dewey who?
Dewey have to give the dog a bath?

Knock-knock.
Who's there?
Yvonne.
Yvonne who?
Yvonne to see my pet turtle?

Knock-knock.
Who's there?
America.
America who?
America is more fun than a sad cur.

Knock-knock.
Who's there?
Vinnie.
Vinnie who?
Vinnie you gonna let me get a dog?

Knock-knock.
Who's there?
Wicked.
Wicked who?
Wicked get dogs instead of having kids.

Knock-knock.
Who's there?
Butcher.
Butcher who?
Butcher mouse in the snake's mouth and
    watch what happens!

Knock-knock.
Who's there?
Justice.
Justice who?
Justice I thought! You put a frog under my pillow!

Knock-knock.
Who's there?
Vera.
Vera who?
Vera you gonna put the fish tank?

Knock-knock.
Who's there?
Candy.
Candy who?
Candy vet fix my dog's broken foot?

Knock-knock.
Who's there?
Wilma.
Wilma who?
Wilma poor lost doggie ever come home?

Knock-knock.
Who's there?
Mitzi.
Mitzi who?
Mitzi cage door shut, the cat will never get the canary.

Knock-knock.
Who's there?
Cereal.
Cereal who?
Cereal kick owning a skunk.

Knock-knock.
Who's there?
Gopher.
Gopher who?
Gopher a walk with the dog, would you?

Knock-knock.
Who's there?
Earl.
Earl who?
Earl be happy to walk the dog, Mama!

Knock-knock.
Who's there?
Luke.
Luke who?
Luke both ways before you cross the street
    with the chicken!

Knock-knock.
Who's there?
Detail.
Detail who?
Detail of the rabbit is in back.

Knock-knock.
Who's there?
Police.
Police who?
Police, Dad, can I have a horse?

Knock-knock.
Who's there?
Wanda.
Wanda who?
Wanda go catch some frogs?

Knock-knock.
Who's there?
Egypt.
Egypt who?
Egypt you when he sold you a dead parrot.

Knock-knock.
Who's there?
Oooze.
Ooze who?
Ooze going to teach my dog some tricks?

Knock-knock.
Who's there?
Wendy.
Wendy who?
Wendy dog has to go out, it scratches on the
    door.

Knock-knock.
Who's there?
Freighter.
Freighter who?
Freighter snakes? You bet I am!

Knock-knock.
Who's there?
Roxanne.
Roxanne who?
Roxanne coral make nice fish tank
  decorations.

Knock-knock.
Who's there?
Handsome.
Handsome who?
Handsome catnip to me and watch the cat
  go crazy!

Knock-knock.
Who's there?
Jester.
Jester who?
Jester minute—I'm teaching my parrot to
  talk.

Knock-knock.
Who's there?
Midas.
Midas who?
Midas well find a ladder so we can get the cat
  out of the tree.

Knock-knock.
Who's there?
Stopwatch.
Stopwatch who?
Stopwatch're doing and feed the cat!

Knock-knock.
Who's there?
Emmett.
Emmett who?
Emmett a man who wanted to sell me his
   beekeeping equipment!

Knock-knock.
Who's there?
Turnip.
Turnip who?
Turnip the tank heat too high and you'll cook
   your fish!

Knock-knock.
Who's there?
Cracker.
Cracker who?
Cracker eggs and the chicken will peck your
   eyes out!

Knock-knock.
Who's there?
Tyrone.
Tyrone who?
Tyrone dog up! Mine is in our yard, where
   he belongs!

A WARM, HOLIDAY CAT STORY

Knock-knock.
Who's there?
Value.
Value who?
Value look after my cat while I'm on vacation?

Knock-knock.
Who's there?
Violet.
Violet who?
Violet your cat out, will you bring me a T-shirt?

Knock-knock.
Who's there?
Lettuce.
Lettuce who?
Lettuce see how well you treat her first.

Knock-knock.
Who's there?
Shelby.
Shelby who?
Shelby fine, I promise!

Knock-knock.
Who's there?
Yul.
Yul who?
Yul never guess what happened while you were gone.

Knock-knock.
Who's there?
York.
York who?
York cat ate my turkey!

Knock-knock.
Who's there?
Sloan.
Sloan who?
Sloan as my kitty's okay, I don't care.

Knock-knock.
Who's there?
Byte.
Byte who?
Byte way ... we ate your cat for
  Thanksgiving.

A FEW MORE PET KNOCK-KNOCKS ...

Knock-knock.
Who's there?
Dwayne.
Dwayne who?
Dwayne the tank, the goldfish is dead.

Knock-knock.
Who's there?
Fuer Elise
Fuer Elise who?
Fuer Elise bit interested in buying a horse,
  I'll give you a good price!

Knock-knock.
Who's there?
Ethel.
Ethel who?
Ethel parrots, in case you want to buy one.

Knock-knock.
Who's there?
Howard.
Howard who?
Howard you like to get me a puppy, Dad?

Knock-knock.
Who's there?
Donna.
Donna who?
Donna sit there or you'll crush the cat.

Knock-knock.
Who's there?
Hyper.
Hyper who?
Hypersonally prefer dogs to cat.

Knock-knock.
Who's there?
Tom Sawyer.
Tom Sawyer who?
Tom Sawyer brother throw a cat in the river.

A LITTLE TALE OF HORSIN' AROUND

Knock-knock.
Who's there?
Rhoda.
Rhoda who?
Rhoda horse for the third time.

Knock-knock.
Who's there?
Muffin.
Muffin who?
Muffin afraid when I ride horses.

Knock-knock.
Who's there?
Sherwood.
Sherwood who?
Sherwood like to say I had a good time on
    the trail, but—

Knock-knock.
Who's there?
Acid.
Acid who?
Acid down on the horse's back and—

Knock-knock.
Who's there?
Weirdo.
Weirdo who?
Weirdo you think the horse went galloping?

Knock-knock.
Who's there?
Forrest.
Forrest who?
Forrest stable!

Knock-knock.
Who's there?
Eyes darted.
Eyes darted who?
Eyes darted to fall off the horse's back!

Knock-knock.
Who's there?
Justin.
Justin who?
Justin time, I grabbed the horse's mane be-
   fore I slid off!

Knock-knock.
Who's there?
Willis.
Willis who?
"Willis horse ever stop galloping?" I yelled.

Knock-knock.
Who's there?
Stu.
Stu who?
Stu late! Guess what happened?

Knock-knock.
Who's there?
Eiffel.
Eiffel who?
Eiffel off the horse anyway.

Knock-knock.
Who's there?
Maybe.
Maybe who?
Maybe hind was sore from the fall.

Knock-knock.
Who's there?
Esther.
Esther who?
"Esther anything I can do to help?" a friend
    asked.

Knock-knock.
Who's there?
Wally.
Wally who?
"Wally you help me get back in the saddle?"
    I replied.

Knock-knock.
Who's there?
Disaster.
Disaster who?
"Disaster be the worst day of my equestrian
    life!" I told him.

Knock-knock.
Who's there?
Dishes.
Dishes who?
Dishes the end of the ride, thank God!

Knock-knock.
Who's there?
Celeste.
Celester who?
Celeste time I'll go horseback riding!

Knock-knock.
Who's there?
Icy.
Icy who?
"Icy why you fell off the horse!" my friend
    said.

Knock-knock.
Who's there?
Avenue.
Avenue who?
"Avenue heard?" he continued. "You're
    supposed to ride with a saddle!"

Knock-knock.
Who's there?
Albee.
Albee who?
"Albee darned!" I replied. "I didn't know
    that."

Knock-knock.
Who's there?
Hacienda.
Hacienda who?
Hacienda the horse story.

A VERY SHORT AND DIRTY DOG TALE

Knock-knock.
Who's there?
Pudding.
Pudding who?
Pudding shoes on to walk the dog is a
   bother, Ma!

Knock-knock.
Who's there?
Saul.
Saul who?
Saul over your foot! Haven't I told you not to
   walk the dog barefoot?

A FISHY FISH TALE

Knock-knock.
Who's there?
Yacht.
Yacht who?
Yacht to know what I want for my birthday,
   Mom!

Knock-knock.
Who's there?
Olaf.
Olaf who?
Olaf these years I've been asking for
  goldfish.

Knock-knock.
Who's there?
Final.
Final who?
Final get you some!

Knock-knock.
Who's there?
Abbott.
Abbott who?
Abbott you the goldfish, but I forgot to get a
  bowl.

Knock-knock.
Who's there?
Warren.
Warren who?
Warren the world have you been keeping
  them?

Knock-knock.
Who's there?
Indy.
Indy who?
Indy upstairs bathroom.

Knock-knock.
Who's there?
Godson.
Godson who?
Godson bad news for you!

Knock-knock.
Who's there?
Diploma.
Diploma who?
Diploma came and let the water out of the
    bathtub!

AND FINALLY ...

Knock-knock.
Who's there?
Snow.
Snow who?
Snow more animal jokes in this book!

There's an epidemic with 27 million victims. And no visible symptoms.

It's an epidemic of people who can't read.

Believe it or not, 27 million Americans are functionally illiterate, about one adult in five.

The solution to this problem is you... when you join the fight against illiteracy. So call the Coalition for Literacy at toll-free 1-800-228-8813 and volunteer.

Volunteer Against Illiteracy.
The only degree you need is a degree of caring.